A Clever Title Goes Here

Mordechai Schmutter

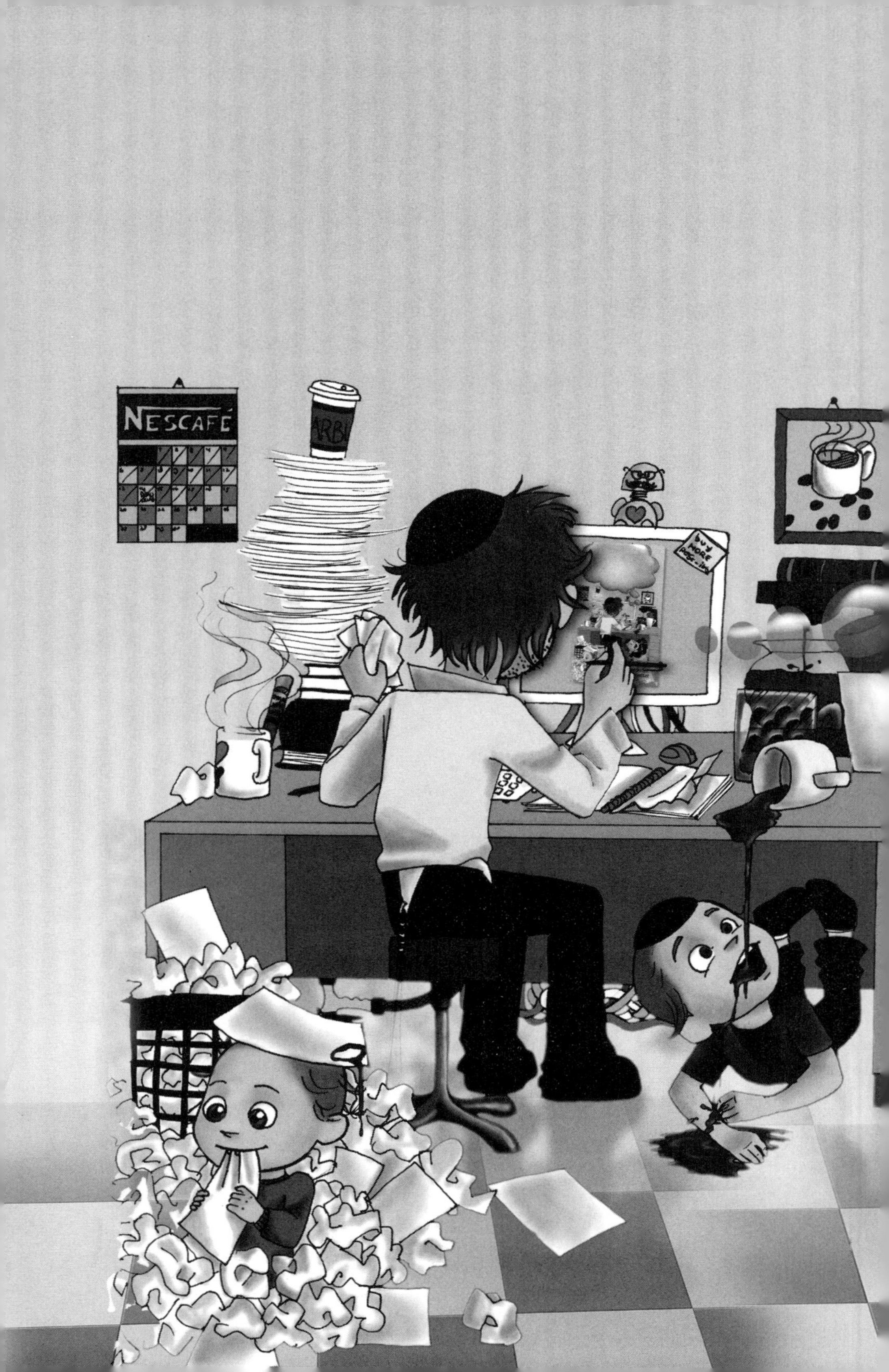
NESCAFÉ

A Clever Title Goes Here

ISRAEL BOOKSHOP PUBLICATIONS

Mordechai Schmutter

Copyright © 2009 by Mordechai Shmutter

ISBN 978-1-60091-116-3

All Rights Reserved

No part of this book may be reproduced in any form
without written permission from the copyright holder.
The Rights of the Copyright Holder Will Be Strictly Enforced

Book & Cover design by:
vividesign
SRULY PERL • 845.694.7186

Distributed by:
ISRAEL BOOKSHOP PUBLICATIONS
501 Prospect Street, Lakewood, NJ 08701
Tel: (732) 901-3009
Fax: (732) 901-4012
www.israelbookshoppublications.com
info@israelbookshoppublications.com

Printed in the USA

To all of my readers
(You know who you are)

Table of Contents

Acknowledgements..11
Introduction..13

Happy Now?

My Very First Article...25
Some Cutting Remarks..30
How Old Are You Now...35
Unbounded *Simchah*...40
Too Much Soda...45
Dancing Backward..50
Unabashed...55

Running With Scissors

Road Trip Advice for People Who Don't Know Better...............65
Writing Home..71
Time to Think...76
Shmoozing About Snoozing..81
Caution: Kids at Work...86

Tuition Break

Supplies!...74
Living in the Projects..100

Open House...105
Teachers Are Parents Too..110
You Must Be This Tall To Wait In Line.....................115

Not Rocket Science

Losing RAM...125
How Ignoble of You..130
A Sense of Academia...135

Chicken Soup For The Stomach

Bursting With Flavor..145
Mineral Coke...150
How Do You Like *Them* Apples?...............................155
On Display...160

Taking it With You

Cheaper Living..169
Even Cheaper Living..174
Full of Hot Air..179
Promising the Moon..185
Gastronomical...190

There's No "Nun" In "Yuntiff"

Relaxing is Cleaning, Too..199
Food For Thought...204
Stop and Smell the Parsley.......................................209
Sukkah Basics...215
Dreidel for Dummies: An Instruction Manual............221
Oy, Gevalt! I Almost Forgot!.....................................227

Acknowledgements

"Where's my *Shamash*?"..232
This Article Has a Theme...237
A Freilichen Purim, Osama: A Purim Shpiel..................242

Asking For Trouble

Numbers, People!..255
Caution: No Signs Ahead..260
When Facing Muggers, Always Carry a Handkerchief........265
Mooving Around..270
No Laughing Matter...275
It's All the Rage...281

Adventures In Columnism

Mabul in the Garage..291
Nearsighted..296
Shoeless and Beltless...301
Six Pretzels..306
Sharing Our Time...311
Mainly Airborne..316

Who Is He?

I am Who I Am...325
Glossary..331

Acknowledgements

There are a lot of people without whom I could not have written this book, but I hope you won't hold it against them. They're all very nice people, and they couldn't have known how it would turn out.

- My wife, for always providing encouragement in the form of reading my articles and going, "That's it? You already told me all these jokes!"

- My parents, who didn't panic when I told them I wanted to be a writer. Granted, when I was six I told them I wanted to be a babysitter, so "writer" was at least closer to what they had in mind for me. But it was no "accountant".

- My kids, for letting me realize my dream of being a babysitter, and for always being there. While I'm trying to write.

- My in-laws, for not meeting me until my wife was already pretty sure she was going to marry me, and for always providing encouragement in the form of sending me job ads upwards of six times a week since I got married — for jobs that are not always related to my line of work, but that are conveniently located within driving distance of their home.

- To Mr. Kaufman, Mrs. Delmar, and all of the people at Israel Book Shop, for taking me under their wings before anyone had even heard of me, and agreeing to publish a book with no plot and very little research to back it up, and are now, with my second book, helping me venture into the genre of Books That Don't Even Stick To One Topic For More Than About Three Pages At A Time.

- The people at Hamodia, and especially Mrs. Frankfurter, Mrs. Ehrlich, Mrs. Hubner, and all of the people above them whom they're afraid to let me talk to, for agreeing to give a regular weekly humor column to a relative unknown, despite all common sense telling them that I would probably run their entire newspaper to the ground.

- Chaim Kaufman, for taking my calls at all hours of the day and night so we could schmooze about totally random subjects that I may or may not write about. And especially for the times (this happens almost every week) when I call him in a panic to say, "I'm in middle of writing an article and I only have six hundred words! And no topic!"

- To all of the people who submitted possible titles for this book. If I could have used all of them, I would have, but then it would have taken forever to ask for it in a bookstore.

Most of all, I would like to thank the *Ribono shel Olam* for getting me to this point, and for creating a world in which there are so many great things to make jokes about.

Introduction

People often ask me about the kind of work and dedication it takes to write a humor column. Actually, those aren't their exact words. Their exact words are: "Any weirdo can write this nonsense!" So I think it's very important that you know right off the bat that it takes a very specific *type* of weirdo to write this nonsense.

For one thing, when you're writing humor, you never really know if it's funny. Sure, *you* think it's funny, but that doesn't mean anything. A lot of people think their own jokes are funny, but most of the time they're not. We all know someone who is always making jokes and laughing hysterically over them, and we have to pretend to laugh along because we don't have the heart to tell him that it's always the same three jokes.

So how do you know if what you write is any good? You can show it to your family and friends, who will tell you, under intense interrogation, that it was really good, but that could be because they don't want to hurt your feelings, or get into a long extended conversation about *why* it's not good. Because if they tell you *why* it's not good, you're just going to write *another* draft, and you'll make them read that one, too, and they really don't want to because they're pretty sure that that one's not going to be good either. So what they do instead is they say that it's "really good", which is the same thing that you say if someone asks if you need help with something that you would rather handle on your own.

You say, "No thanks, I'm really good." So in essence, these people are telling you to leave them alone.

So how do you tell if they really mean it? How did all of the great writers, such as William Shakespeare and Charles Dickens (and by "great" I mean "lived a long time ago," as in "great-great-grandfather"), figure out if people really liked their work, or if they were just being nice because they didn't want to be forced to read any more sentences that they had to repeat three or four times out loud before they got any glimmer of an idea of what the writer was talking about?

One method you can use is to write two pieces. You give them the first piece, ask for their opinion (of course they will say that it's "really good"), and then you bring out the second piece and see if their expression changes. In fact, you don't even have to write a whole second piece. You can just write one page, or even just a cover page, and then staple it to a stack of paper the size of a phone book. Then pay attention to see if they're eager to read it, or if they suddenly make up some dental appointment that they're supposed to go to, even though it's a Sunday afternoon. Most writers find that this is the best way to do it. In fact, Dostoyevsky did this all the time, which explains the size of *War and Peace*.

On the other hand, if what you're writing is humor, there's a very easy way to see if people like it – just hang back and see if they actually laugh while they're reading it, or if they sit there in stony silence like they're at the Department of Motor Vehicles – basically, just waiting for the piece to be over – and then, as soon as they finish, turn to you and say, "It was really good. Really."

So based on this, you'd think that writing a humor column is easy, because all you have to do is show it to someone and see if he

Introduction

laughs. But it's still not simple, because the other big problem with writing a weekly humor column is that you have to write one every single week, which means that no matter what you're doing at any given moment, there will always be a massive deadline looming over you. Sometimes you'll just be sitting there, minding your own business, and meanwhile the deadline is sneaking up behind you, moving closer and closer, until you turn around and shriek, "Oh, my goodness, I don't have a topic yet!"

So most of your columns get written very close to the deadline – some of them as close as one day after the deadline – and you don't always have time to find people to read it.

"But what about your spouse?" you will ask.

Here's the thing: No matter how funny you are, your spouse knows you like the back of her hand, and will almost never laugh at your jokes. If you ask me, this isn't fair, because back when you were dating, she laughed at *everything*, and you were like, "Wow, we're connecting on so many levels!" But now you're pretty sure she was just laughing so you'd want to marry her. But in the meantime, she's insisting that now that she knows you better, she can actually anticipate every joke you're going to say before you even say it, because your relationship has matured.

(This is the third biggest hurdle when it comes to humor writing: maturity.)

Also, when you're writing a humor column, you never really know where the humor is going to come from. You could go skydiving for the express purpose of coming up with something to write about, and not have anything funny happen the whole time, *baruch Hashem*, and then, when you're on your way home, wondering what on earth you're going to write about now that you just wasted the whole day not writing, you all of a sudden get stuck in traffic, and you realize that that's your topic – traffic. There was one week that I was sitting in front of the computer for the better part of a day, trying to come up with something to write about, and the whole time my kids were coming over to me and bothering me for snacks. So I'd get up and give them snacks, and five minutes later they'd come back. "We're still hungry," they'd say. Like there's any way that I, as a semi-responsible parent, would give them enough potato chips to actually make them full. But I couldn't concentrate on coming up with a topic because the whole time they were bothering me for food, and then I realized: That's the topic. So I wrote about kids who try to stave off boredom by bothering their parents for food.

My point is, that as a writer trying to write columns about everyday life, you always have deadlines, and sometimes you're so busy trying to *make* those deadlines, that you're not actually living out your everyday life, and then you're wondering why you can't make those deadlines.

The other thing about humor is that what seems hysterical to one person might actually be un-funny or even upsetting to another person. Most of the time, when I come up with a topic, I don't bother running it by the newspaper editors first, because I'm always afraid they're going to nix it for one reason or another. The newspaper I write for has a reputation for being a very serious paper, and I'm always afraid that one day they're going to come to their senses. So I usually just write it up and send it in, and then hope that they're so far behind deadline that they'll let my article in just to fill the page.

Introduction

But sometimes there are issues. For example, the other week I wrote an article about fighting obesity.

Now, before I get a whole bunch of angry letters, I want to stress that the article was about fighting *obesity*, not about fighting *obese people*. Obese people are generally some of the nicest people around, and there's never any reason to fight them ~~especially when you can just outrun them~~. And besides, I myself am one-quarter obese. Not only that, but the article was about the fact that we're *all* fat, and about how we, as a society could lose weight together. And not by carpooling to the gym.

But then, when I opened the magazine on the week that the article was supposed to appear, I saw that the editors had instead inserted the article that was slated to appear the *following* week. So I wrote them an e-mail, asking why they didn't run the obesity article. Were they afraid of offending people who wouldn't realize that I was poking fun at society as a whole, rather than at specific people? Were they afraid of upsetting some of their advertisers, such as the ice cream companies and the all-the-matzah-you-can-eat Pesach hotels?

So my editor wrote back to tell me that the magazine, which I almost never have the time to read, seeing as I'm always behind deadline, had a huge feature that week on anorexia. So at the last minute, they decided to pull my column, because they couldn't have people read an article about the seriousness of anorexia, and then turn the page for an article making fun of being fat. ("I can't eat; I can't starve myself; what am I supposed to do?")

But my point is that when you're writing humor, you have to be careful not to offend anyone, and sometimes this doesn't just mean writing jokes that are okay, but also knowing when you can or can't make those jokes.

So mainly, this book is a product of me sitting in front of my computer and guessing what people are going to laugh about, and then showing the final product to my wife and watching her roll her eyes, and then sending it to my editors and hoping they'll like it.

Which brings us to the title.

It's very hard to come up with a book title. You want a title that says something about the book, but of course it can't say too much. For example, if you're writing a mystery novel, you can't call your book *The Main Character's Friend Did It for the Insurance Money*. But you also can't call it *101 Fat-Free Recipes Made Mainly From Twigs*. It has to at least have *something* to do with the book.

But therein lay the conundrum: This book is a compilation of dozens of articles on all different topics. What do you call a book when there is no one topic that it's about, where the only thing the articles in it have in common is that they're all written in the same basic style, and that about half of them seem to involve goats?

So after hours of thinking about it—in bed, while driving, during the rabbi's speech, while my wife was doing housework ("Mordechai, come help me bring out the garbage." "I can't, I'm thinking about it.")—I finally decided that the best thing to do would be to take the responsibility off myself, and let the readers decide. So I wrote a column announcing that I was holding a Book Title Contest, and that people could write in with title suggestions for a chance at winning a free signed copy of the book (unless they didn't want me

Introduction

to ruin it by writing in it). Surprisingly, I got hundreds of responses, and a lot of them were really good.

However, I got the feeling that some people didn't really understand how the contest was going to work. One woman wrote, "I never win *anything*," which is exactly what *I* say when people ask me why I don't play the lottery. Another person suggested a title that compared my name to a rag used to clean floors. This led me to believe that some of my readers thought that I was going to draw the title out of a hat, and that whatever title came out, no matter how really good or insulting it was, was going to be the title I would plaster right on the front of the book to convince people to buy it. It got to the point where I was actually afraid to pick a title, because I figured people would sneer at it and say, "Yeah, he only picked that one because it was the best."

So I narrowed it down to a few options that I was able to live with (the ones that were *really* really good), and sent them to my publisher: "Here. *You* pick one." And my publisher promptly sent me a letter in return: "I don't *wanna* pick one! *You* pick one!" And this went back and forth for a while, and in the meantime the deadline snuck up on us, and we ended up with just the placeholder words that we'd put on the cover to let us know where the title would go if we ever ended up picking one.

Okay, so that's not really what happened. "A Clever Title Goes Here" was actually the name of the original article in which I'd announced the Title Contest, and one of my readers, Yankel Friedman of Brooklyn (and it's not my fault that his name sounds made up), wrote in to say, "Hey! Why don't you just use *that* as a title?" And then, when I sent that title, among many others, to my publisher, the publisher said, "Yeah! Why *don't* you just use that as a title?" And it turns out I didn't have a good reason why not to. So here we are.

So now Yankel Friedman of Brooklyn is going to receive a free signed copy of my book, for essentially pointing out that I'd already come up with my own title. Thanks a lot, Yankel!

But the joke's on him. The book is full of articles that he's probably read already.

However, this title is not without benefits:

    a. No one has any idea what it means, but on the other hand,

    b. No one has any idea what the rest of the book means, either, so really it sums the book up nicely, and

    c. If you can get past the corniness of the title, the rest of the book should be smooth sailing.

So now that *that's* out of the way, you might as well read the book. It's really good.

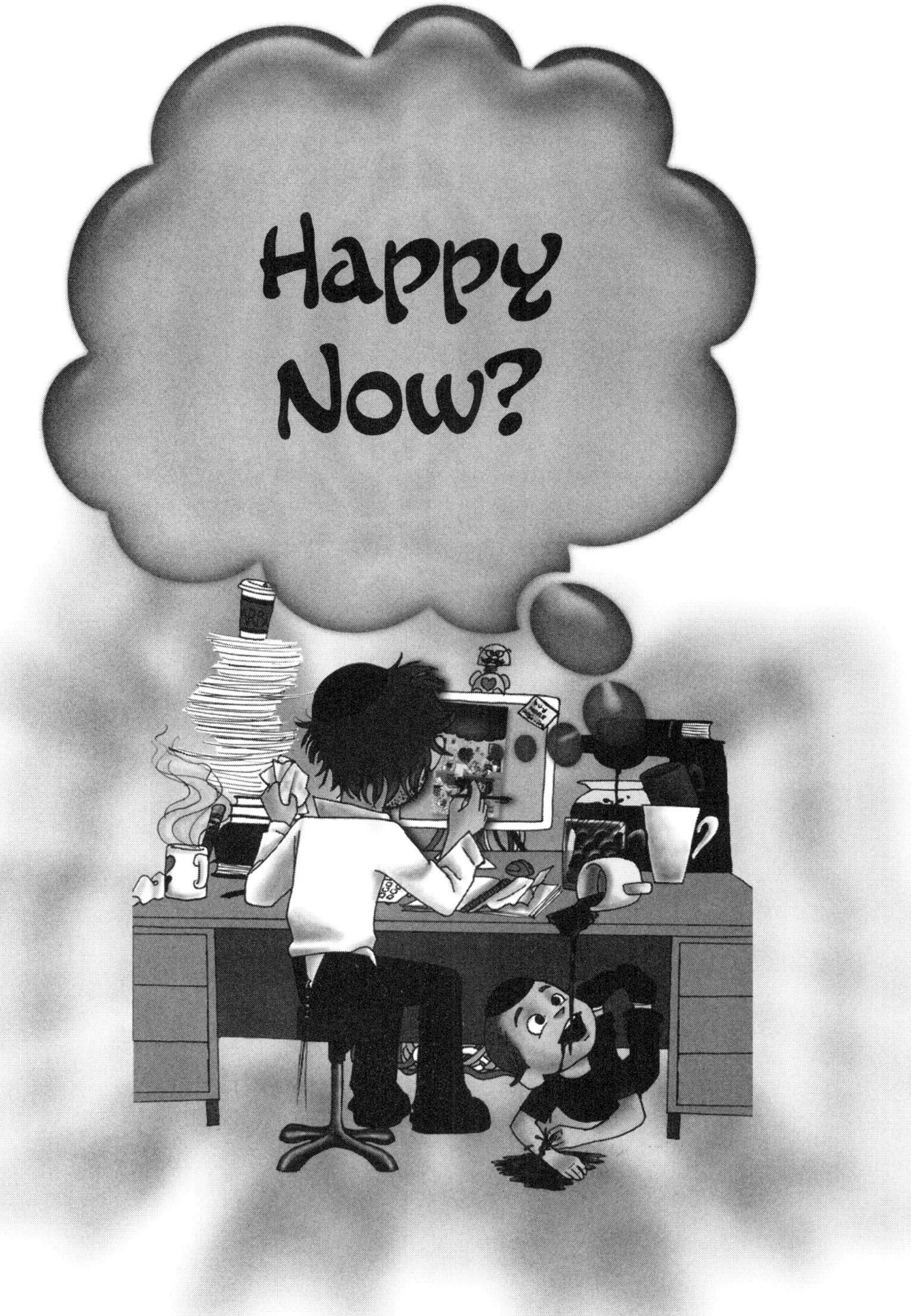
Happy
Now?

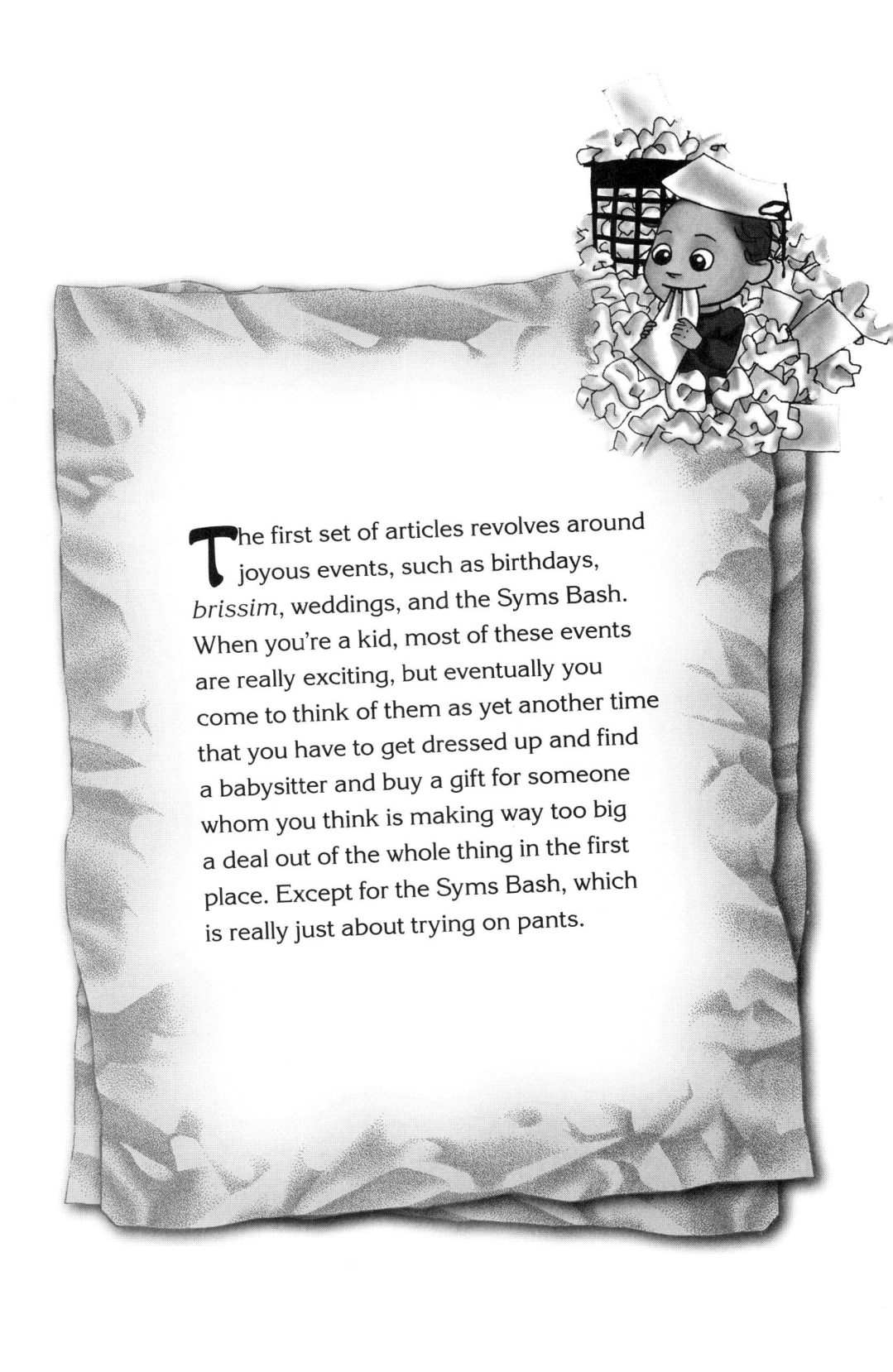

The first set of articles revolves around joyous events, such as birthdays, *brissim*, weddings, and the Syms Bash. When you're a kid, most of these events are really exciting, but eventually you come to think of them as yet another time that you have to get dressed up and find a babysitter and buy a gift for someone whom you think is making way too big a deal out of the whole thing in the first place. Except for the Syms Bash, which is really just about trying on pants.

I recently came across the very first humor article that I ever wrote. It seems to be in journal form. I'm so glad I've matured since then.

Anyway, here goes:

DAY 1: Whew, what a long day! Let's see: First I was born—that's always a big deal—and then I met this older couple—older than me, anyway. The man looks a little like me, but hairier, and his wife looks—well, she looks tired. (I think I might be their first, because the man seemed afraid that he was going to drop me.) I also got to meet my doctor, and a whole slew of nurses, and the guy who cleans the delivery room. The nurses gave me a free hat, in blue—that's just my color—plus I got this bracelet with all of my information on it. I wish I knew what it said. I'm going to find out if any of these other babies know how to read.

DAY 2: Still tired from the move. There's not much to do here, plus they've got me all bundled up in a blanket. And when am I getting some pants? I tried crying for them earlier, but the nurses didn't seem to understand me. Some professionals they are. Mommy said we were going to go for a walk, but she ended up just pushing my bed around the hospital. Am I some kind of prisoner here? I don't even remember doing anything. Why is there a theft tag around my ankle? Oops, I think it just fell off again.

DAY 3: I finally got some pants. They came with socks already attached. I think this means we're going home. The nurses tell Mommy that we can leave as soon as they process her paperwork, which should take about five or ten minutes. Mommy says that she wasn't born yesterday. Neither was I!

DAY 4: I went to shul for the first time today. They made me sit in the women's section, which I didn't like, because I wanted to *bentch gomel.*

DAY 5: I am officially the cutest baby ever. This has been confirmed by both of my parents and at least two aunts. But I sure wish everyone would stop squeezing me so much.

DAY 6: Got a sponge bath today. Tatty bought me a towel with a hood on it. I guess that's in case I go outside in my towel, and it starts raining.

DAY 7: Mommy and Tatty seem very busy today. They're buying bagels, setting up platters, and cutting melons. They even bought me a yarmulka that ties under my chin. How come Tatty's yarmulka doesn't tie under *his* chin? Also, a rabbi came by and said Shema with me, and he got a *pekeleh*. I think we're having some kind of party tomorrow.

DAY 8: Oh.

DAY 10: Still tired from the party. I've never had so much wine in my life. That was a *good* napkin. Did anyone catch my name? I didn't hear it; I was screaming the whole time. And no one is actually using it; they're still calling me "the baby". I guess I'll find out the first time I get an *aliyah*.

DAY 11: Someone put a bear in my crib that's twice my size, and they wonder why I spend half the night screaming.

DAY 12: I think I like this middle-of-the-night feeding thing. I get my parents all to myself, and they have no distractions or anything. I'm going to have to do this more often.

DAY 13: I lost my belly button thingy. Seriously. I have no idea where it is. I'd retrace my steps, but I haven't taken any. Who would steal a belly button thingy? I hope my belly button still works without it.

DAY 14: Everyone talks to me like I'm mentally challenged. What exactly is a "googoo-gaga"?

DAY 15: "Hi" is another big word for grownups. "Hi." "Hi." "Hi." Okay, I get it. Can we move on?

DAY 16: And what's with this rattle they keep waving in my face? That can get annoying. Are those beans inside that thing? As soon as I learn to crawl, I'm going to crack that thing open and eat the beans.

DAY 17: I think I'm getting bigger. I just went up a size. I suspect it's because I drink so much and never really get exercise. I need to get an exersaucer.

DAY 18: What exactly is in formula? Why does it smell like that? What's with the aftertaste? Personally, I prefer Kiddush wine.

DAY 19: Mommy taught me a new song. It's called "Rock-a-bye Baby". It's about a baby in a cradle hanging from a tree branch on a windy day, and it doesn't end well. And now I'm supposed to fall asleep?

DAY 20: Tatty put me on the phone with Bubby today. I didn't say much, but she didn't exactly say anything of note, either. She basically said "Hi" a lot, and then asked me, "Who's a little *zeeskeit*?" I don't know, Bubby; I haven't been around the block enough times. Why don't you tell me, so I know what to answer next time?

DAY 21: Mommy and I went to the doctor. Mommy drove. The doctor examined me, and then asked her if I respond normally to sounds. I didn't hear what she answered, because I was busy listening to the people talking in the next room, and to the car backfiring outside. The latter scared me, so I started crying, and no one knew why. Maybe the adults should get *their* hearing checked. After that, the doctor gave me a shot, and remarked about how well I'd behaved. Of course I behaved. When I saw the huge needle in your hand, I had no idea you were going to lunge at me with it. I haven't been around the block yet, remember? Next time, you *bet* I'm going to cry. I may even spit up on your shoes. But I got a Snoopy band-aid, so everything makes sense again.

DAY 22: My parents put a lot of toys in my crib to keep me busy. Busy, busy, busy. I hardly have time for writing anymore.

DAY 25: I learned how to hold my own head up today. There's not much to it. It's like riding a bike.

DAY 26: Spent a lot of the day crying. No one knew why. They kept passing me back and forth: "Is he hungry?" "Is he tired?" "Does he need a diaper?" No. I need a cookie.

DAY 27: Tatty gave me a pacifier. I tried sucking, but there was nothing in it. It's like that time I tried sucking my thumb. There was nothing in that, either.

DAY 28: I finally went for a walk around the block. It's overrated. I don't know anything now that I did not know before that isn't *lashon hara*.

DAY 29: More platters. It looks like we're getting ready for another party. Hmm.

DAY 30: Turns out one of those platters was for me. I now officially have a last name, too, although I didn't get to hear it, because I was busy putting sugar cubes in my mouth.

DAY 31: All in all, even though not everything my parents do is completely logical to me right now, the main thing is that they mean well, and they always have my best interests at heart. Maybe instead of trying to second-guess them at every turn, I should at least try to humor them. After all, they did bring me into this world.

DAY 32: Googoo-gaga.

Some Cutting Remarks

One of the first things that you learn as a parent is that children are not very conducive to your sleep. I remember when my son Daniel was born. Actually, I only remember part of it, because I was asleep for most of the birth. But it wasn't my fault. We had gone to the hospital at two in the morning, and Daniel was not born until eight. My feeling was that if he was going to be born at eight, we should not have left for the hospital until at least seven-thirty. That way we (by which I mean I) could have been nice and rested, and not almost miss everything because I was trying to get some sleep on that little two-person couch in the delivery room.

I had another bout of sleep deprivation recently, when I was trying to put together Daniel's *upsherin* party. I got to bed very late the night before, which was a Motza'ei Shabbos, and I had a dream wherein I was still cooking and cleaning and setting up the party when the sun came up, and all of the guests were arriving, and I no longer had time to go to sleep. And then I woke up. There's nothing more tiring than going to sleep and having a dream wherein you don't get to go to sleep.

Personally, I blame our stove. Our stove had broken down the previous week, and although we'd called the company on Monday morning, they did not actually send anybody until Friday afternoon, about a half-hour before Shabbos, and all the warning that we got came from a phone call from the repairman fifteen minutes earlier that he was in the neighborhood. This struck me as weird, because I assumed that it was the repairman's job to be in the neighborhood -- not that he would be dropping off his dry-cleaning anyway, and deciding that once he was here he would give us a call. Nevertheless, the implication of his call was that if we said, "No thanks, it's almost Shabbos," then he would not be "in the neighborhood" again until the next time we had to cook for an *upsherin*. So we welcomed him in, and told him that he had twenty minutes, and so the first thing he did, upon coming into the kitchen, was play around with the knobs and blow all the power. He then spent ten minutes fiddling with it before leaving, saying he would have to "order new parts". We haven't seen him since. But that is not the point. The point is that my wife spent the entire Motza'ei Shabbos camped out at someone else's house, boiling pot after pot of noodles, and we didn't get started on anything else until late.

But we did have some help. My mother showed up at the party with, among other things, a plate of black-and-white cookies decorated to look like little boys with haircuts. She'd made faces on the white halves, decorated the black halves to look like yarmulkes, and topped it off with two twirly Super Snacks dipped in chocolate to look like *peyos*. The cookies were very pretty, so no one ate them. Or maybe no one wanted to think about mixing chocolate with Super Snacks.

In the early planning stages of the party, I, too, had wanted to make a theme. I was going to give out cheap combs and crazy-hair candy and serve angel-hair pasta -- and then I ran out of ideas for foods with the word "hair" in them. So we didn't end up with a theme. But by the end of the party, most of the foods had hair in them, anyway. (Although we never did end up playing "Pin the Ponytail on the Donkey".)

Then there was the matter of planning the actual ceremony. I didn't remember much from my brothers' *upsherins*, aside from the fact that every guest got to chop off a piece, and that by the time they were done, my brothers looked like they were attacked by beavers, and the professional barbers my father brought them to afterwards wanted to call it in as child abuse. "How many people did you say did this to him?"

So I looked up the reason for the *minhag*, and found that it was based on the *pasuk* that compares a person to a tree. Trees need warmth and sunlight and water and dirt to grow in, and eventually they tower over you and produce fruit. So, too, a little boy needs warmth, and sunlight, and water and dirt to play in, and one day he will tower over you and maybe once in a while eat a piece of fruit. Also, some trees make a mess on your lawn, and eventually fall over and wreck your house.

But that is not the point. The point is that man is compared to a tree, and you're not supposed to cut the fruit off a tree for the first three years of its life – this is called *orlah*. And when you do get around to trimming your field, you're supposed to leave *peyos* for the poor people. So right off, I knew that I was going to have to bring in a massive set of garden scissors for photo ops.

The other part of the *minhag*, I found out, is the fact that, at three, a child is finally old enough for *chinuch*. So we give him *tzitzis* and a yarmulke and help him make *brachos*, and then we teach him the sweetness of the Torah by having him lick honey off a page of the *alef beis* with a lollypop. Some families have a *minhag* of giving the child cupcakes with letters of the *alef beis* written on them. Then, after twenty-two cupcakes, everyone has to talk the child out of a tree. (See, there's that tree again.)

I wasn't entirely sure which to do first – the cutting or the *alef beis*, but in hindsight, I don't know if it was the best idea to have him lick honey off a lollypop moments after his haircut. I have no idea how much hair we made him swallow.

Not that there was very much hair to begin with. Everyone took off only a couple of strands, but he probably won't need another haircut for a while, which is just as well, because I think he's going to expect us to make him a party every time now.

All in all, the party went off smoothly. There was plenty of food, and even though I was tired, I did not accidentally nick anyone's ear. We made our first cut from the area where he will someday put on his *tefillin*, and we made the last cut from the area where he will someday cover up his bald spot with his yarmulke. We also left *peyos*, but they did not look like twirly Super Snacks. They looked more like falafel bits, in that they consisted of random swirls and were two different sizes.

And then there was the matter of the hair. I'd heard that some people weigh the hair and give its value to *tzedakah*, and that others give it to an organization that makes wigs for children with cancer. Unfortunately, the amount of hair we cut off Daniel weighed almost nothing, and would not be enough to make a toupee for a sick hamster. So we're weighing all of the pictures we took. But I don't think we can afford to give *that* much.

If there is one thing that everyone has in common, it's that we all have birthdays. Of course, some of us have more birthdays than others. Some people, such as my son Daniel, for instance, can have as many as three birthdays in one year. Daniel had his *upsherin* three months ago, but is now insisting that he's five years old. This bothers my four-year-old daughter to no end. But, to be fair, Daniel really has no concept of time. He still firmly believes that anything that has ever occurred in the history of the world, including his own birth, happened "last night".

"I got a haircut last night," he tells me.

"It's *sefirah*," I tell him. "You had a haircut on your birthday."

"I had a birthday last night," he says.

Children tend to be very excited about their birthdays. This is because children are constantly being told that, when they get older, they can do tons of exciting, grown-up activities and stay up late and understand big-person jokes, which to them means that, on their birthday, they will all of a sudden magically get any and all mother-in-law jokes. (On that note, now that I am finally at a point in my life that I can actually understand mother-in-law jokes, I no longer find them funny.) This is as opposed to actual grown-ups, who try to avoid talking about their birthdays, because each birthday means they are one step closer to "not a spring chicken anymore". Children are so excited about their birthdays that they are constantly making up new ones. "I'm four and three quarters!" they proudly announce. Never mind the fact that they have no idea what a "quarter" is, and that every time they announce their age they envision a big number four accompanied by three twenty-five-cent coins. You will never hear a grown-up do this. "I'm forty-seven and a half!"

Nevertheless, there is a lot of pressure to have a good birthday. In fact, there is a whole song about it. "Happy birthday to you, happy birthday to you." There are no other words in that part of the song. It has a singular purpose, and that is to instruct you, in no uncertain terms, that you'd better have a happy birthday, because we may follow up on it later. But first we're going to sing you the next part of the song, in which we pester you, no less than four times, to tell us how old you are. *Four times.* Out loud. In a singsong voice, followed by the word "now", like any second the answer is going to change. ("Great. Now I'm thirty-two and a fraction.")

How Old Are You Now?

Many people choose to celebrate the occasion of a birthday by throwing a *"seudas hoda'ah"* to celebrate the fact that the birthday person is still able to attend a *seudas hoda'ah*. Of course, different people have different ideas for their *seudas hoda'ah*. Some people's idea of a *seudas hoda'ah* involves sneaking into the birthday person's house and jumping up and yelling "Surprise!" when he comes inside to find out why it looks like no one's there when there are so many cars in the driveway. Others' idea of a *seudas hoda'ah* involves eating a birthday cake on Shabbos that is exactly like the cake they have *every* Shabbos, except that they sing "Happy Birthday" first. And some people's idea of a *seudas hoda'ah* involves a clown and a multi-layer cake and a bouncy house, or a clown trying to carry a multi-layer cake *through* a bouncy house. I think that's the kind of *seudas hoda'ah* I want when I finish my next *mesechta*.

Of course, there are some birthdays that *everyone* celebrates, such as the third birthday (for boys), the twelfth birthday (for girls), the thirteenth birthday (for slightly taller boys), as well as the eightieth, ninetieth, hundredth, and George Washington's Birthday. A big mark of status in the secular world is when people celebrate your birthday two hundred years after you're gone by buying mattresses at half-price.

But everyone at least has a cake. Birthday cakes are a tradition going back at least as far as the Middle Ages (look it up), when the British would bake small items into their cakes, and if, for instance, you found a coin in your piece, it would mean that you'd be wealthy (or at least one coin richer), and if you found a thimble, it would mean that you'd never marry. (How festive!) And if you found half of a worm, it would mean you were in for a bumpy year. This was how they combined the tradition of birthday cake with the tradition of wrapping their presents. I'm guessing that the *sar ha'ofim* tried a similar thing for one of Pharaoh's birthdays, but Pharaoh didn't get the joke, and the guy ended up in prison with a friend of his who did not seal his beverages properly between uses.

Another thing that's very popular around birthdays is the birthday card. Time was, most birthday cards had pictures of flowers on the front ("I didn't buy you flowers, but here is a picture of some!"), and were bought by grandparents, who were into long mushy poems that went something like this:

Like a rose in a meadow, dripping with dew,

Or a fawn in the forest, sighting a gnu,

Or the very first pickle, that's stuck in a jar,

Okay – I doubt that you're reading this far.

The truth is I'm at the pharmacy waiting for my pills,

I figured I'd read through the cards on the sills,

Did I buy this one last year? Who really knows?

I think that one had lilies, and this one has a rose,

But the content of the card is never the crux,

The point is, it conceals this check for five bucks.

Love, Bubby

Nowadays, there are millions of cards to choose from, for any occasion imaginable. You could walk into the store and say, "I'm looking for a birthday card for someone who just turned fifty-four, is marrying off his second daughter, and celebrating the birth of a grandson, and he just found out that he has mono," and the clerk will say, "Do you want regular or belated?"

How Old Are You Now?

I love that there's a whole category of cards for people who remember their loved ones' birthdays after the fact. I'm just like that. I will remember someone's birthday up until the actual day, then it will slip my mind for a day or two, and then I will remember, just in time to say, "I can't believe I missed their birthday *again*!" But sometimes, if I find a really funny belated card, I will specifically wait a day or two just so I'd be able to use it. (NOTE: This may work for *some* people, but for whatever reason, your spouse will not find it funny.)

In short, there are many ways to celebrate birthdays, whether you're "five" or ninety five, or thirty-nine for the fourth time in a row. And so, in the spirit of originality, I would like to wish all of my readers a happy belated birthday.

How old are you now?

Unbounded Simchah

There are certain seasons in the year called "wedding seasons". I apologize for not telling you about them sooner, but I did not even know that there *was* such a thing as a wedding season. I thought that people got married when they found someone they wanted to spend the rest of their lives with and told everyone they'd ever met and picked out matching china. That's what *I* did. I got married in February. It was snowing during my *chuppah*. Actually, as I later found out from both my wife and my mother, it was snowing *on* my *chuppah*, through the little skylight overhead. I had no idea, because I was wearing a winter coat, under which I was wearing a *kittel*, under which I was wearing a suit jacket, under which I was wearing a tie (which had to be black and white, despite the fact that no one could see it), under which I was wearing a shirt, under which were my *tzitzis*, followed by my undershirt, followed by a massive layer of sweat. So I probably wouldn't have noticed if the entire wedding hall blew away in a tornado, leaving me standing there, hatless, trying to finish that long list of names in my pocket.

But now a lot of the people on that list are getting married, apparently, which I guess makes it wedding season, and so we urge all of the *chassanim* and *kallos* out there to remember that, although you have been looking forward to this day ever since you were four years old and people asked you what you wanted to be when you grew up, and you said, "a *kallah*," you still have to remember that the wedding day is not actually the be-all-and-end-all of your life. In fact, life continues long after the wedding, and in the case of some couples, it may seem even longer. It's like when we go on vacation, and we spend months planning every last detail, and when the vacation is finally over, we take off our sunglasses and our digital cameras and our pedometers and we realize that we have not planned one moment of our lives past the vacation. Where do we go from there? Fortunately, in my case, I could go on to write articles about it. But what do most people do? If your parents spend all of their money on a big fancy wedding for you, what will they have left for you to *shnorr* afterwards?

It's crazy these days, the things people are spending money on for their *simchos*. For instance, some people try to forgo the traditional *bentcher* souvenir, and instead hand out a leather-bound *Tefillas Haderech*. Who takes a leather-bound *Tefillas Haderech* with them onto the plane? Do they have to put it in a one-quart zip-lock bag? Why not give out a *Tefillas Haderech* that hangs on a wall, while you're at it? And then there are ice sculptures. It's one thing if the guests are allowed to chip away at the sculptures and put slivers of it into their drinks, but most caterers frown on that, because someone spent hours and hours carving that thing from a big imported iceberg, rather than just pour ice into a huge plastic mold, which is what you or I would have done. And it's not like everyone could afford to make *simchos* like this either, and more and more parents are finding themselves selling their spare organs to pay for weddings. This is especially tough on people with ten children or more, so something has to be done, or else a lot of parents will find themselves being carried down the aisle in a little plastic baggie. So there are definitely areas in which we can cut back.

For instance, we can cut back on some of the food. The average wedding today serves enough food to render every single new suit and rented gown at the hall at least three sizes too small. In general, the meal should probably consist of the five basic Jewish food groups, which are challah, fish, soup, chicken, and dessert. There can also be a modest "*shmorg*", by which we mean a *shmorg* that does not feature people in funny hats who seem to have forgotten to make the food before the actual wedding began, because they are clearly making it right there at the *shmorg*, and have a long line of people waiting for them while clutching their plates and making awkward conversation with the people behind them who they don't plan on speaking to until at least the next *simchah*. And there is definitely no need for a Viennese table, because even though everyone attacks it like it's the last bus out of the Catskills, the truth is that tomorrow morning they're going to resent you for providing the temptation.

Another example is bands. A lot of people like to go with big bands in huge orchestra pits, with trombones and cymbals and one guy who makes his entire living sitting in the corner with a triangle. But the truth is that every *chasunah* band since the beginning of time plays the same five songs, and it doesn't really matter if it's a one-man band, so long as his amplifier is loud enough to cover for it. Also, you want to make sure that your one man is a keyboard player, rather than the triangle guy. In fact, sometimes it doesn't even matter if there *is* a band, because at various times the *chassan's* friends, who are much louder than the band once they've hit the open bar (another bad idea), will start singing an entirely different song than the one the band is playing, and by the time the band has caught up, they will have moved on to yet a *different* song.

Of course, there are exceptions to every rule. For instance, sometimes it is not a waste of money to have a Viennese table, because the *chassan* is in fact Viennese, and if you don't have a Viennese table, you will not have any table at all. Or maybe the *mechutanim* have come to the agreement that they'd just have a Viennese table *instead* of a main course. After all, candy is cheaper than meat. And sometimes you can get a really huge band from a band *gemach* or something. But everyone should definitely keep one eye on their bank accounts.

But none of this has anything to do with the *chassan*. I remember that before my wedding, the one job that I had, aside from keeping my parents and in-laws apart, was figuring out the *kibbudim* – whom to give which *brachos* to and so on. This took me the entire engagement period. I'm still not sure why.

Which brings me to my own money-saving idea, which is that the *chassan* does all of the planning himself. The *kallah* can have whatever jobs the *chassan* had previously, such as remembering to get dressed up and figuring out the *kibbudim*. And both sets of parents can help her with that. But everything else must be left to the *chassan*.

If the *chassan* plans the wedding himself, there will be nothing there that cannot actually be eaten, such as centerpieces, or even necessarily place cards, and some people will inadvertently not make it to the guest list, such as the *kallah's* grandparents, and there most probably will not be any napkins. Or tablecloths, for that matter.

If this plan is put into effect, people would save a whole lot of money, and weddings would be less about agonizing over what you cannot afford and more about laughing over what the *chassan* forgot this time. "Is there a hall? We have 400 people sitting out in the street! Where do they go?"

This is why we have to get married.

My sister, Faigy (not her real name), recently got engaged, and I decided that it was my job, as her older brother, to educate her *chassan* in the perils of having a humor columnist as a brother-in-law.

"Say something funny," would be my first words to him, at his *l'chaim*. "I'm behind deadline."

I was going to take full advantage of this *l'chaim*, seeing as I had to put on a tie for this, as well as shave on a day that did not end in "Friday". But at least it would be better than what I said to my other brother-in-law at *his l'chaim*:

"Wow, you're tall!"

I am generally not sensitive about my height, because even though I had a short childhood (meaning that *I* was short -- my childhood was regular length, although my wife will insist that it *still* hasn't ended), for the past few years I have basically thought of myself as "about six feet tall", which is how adult males classify themselves if they are anywhere between 5' 8" and 6' 5". About half the people I know are taller than me, and half are shorter. But my brother-in-law is *way* taller. He is one of those people who always has to stand in the back in wedding photos. And he's always the first to know when it rains.

My family always blamed the Havdalah candle. For years, my now-married sister Raizel always held the Havdalah candle as high as she could, because they say that the height of the candle is going to determine the height of your *chassan*. They also say that if you drink Havdalah wine, you grow facial hair. So while I was always drinking Havdalah wine, desperately trying to grow facial hair (I was short, so I figured I should have *something*), Raizel was holding the Havdalah candle way up high, and she got a really tall husband. Whereas I still have patches where I can't grow hair.

So there I was, all excited to meet Faigy's *chassan*, Alter, and to say what I was dying to say to him, and to make a better first impression than I had with my other brother-in-law (or at least a *different* first impression), and the first words out of my mouth when I saw him were:

"Wow, he's even taller!"

Faigy is taller than Raizel, so she, by definition, held the candle higher. There is actually a brown mark on the ceiling of my parents' kitchen right over where they make Havdalah. (This is not a joke. All the people at the *l'chaim* got to see it.) I think my sisters have some kind of contest going to see whose husband knocks into the front-hallway chandelier the most times when he comes to visit my parents. In fact, my parents probably should have taken down the chandelier before the *l'chaim*, because Alter has a *lot* of relatives.

My parents hosted the *l'chaim*, and it was very nice. They even got those fancy chocolates where you don't know what *brachah* they are until after you bite into them. Is it chocolate? Is it cake? That one is shaped like a strawberry; does that mean there's a strawberry *in* it?

And I never know what to do at these things. As the *kallah's* brother, I have to stick around for a while, but I can't just stand around staring into space, and having mundane, filler conversations was not helping me come up with a topic for my article, and if I keep eating those chocolate things my buttons will start popping off and hitting innocent bystanders. So what I generally do is I walk around with a cup of soda (usually ginger ale, which has the side benefit of looking like champagne, which is classier than orange soda), and I just kind of observe the crowd, trying to catch bits and pieces of human behavior, and if someone gets me into a conversation that I think is lasting too long and I want to get back to eavesdropping – sorry, *observing*, -- I just gulp down my soda and excuse myself to go get more. By the end of the night, I've had so much ginger ale that I can't even *look* at it until the next *simchah*.

This *simchah*, unfortunately, did not have any ginger ale, but they did have a bottle of Dr. Pepper, which of course has caffeine, and also exploded when I opened it. This happens to me at every *simchah*. And the fancy party napkins aren't very absorbent at all, so I pretty much had to use up all of the attractive napkin displays, because my parents, while setting up the house for the *simchah*, had hidden the paper towels.

But the truth is that no one really knows what to do at these *simchos*. Everyone seems to have their own routines, which they fall back on at every *simchah* they go to:

- There are the *kallah's* friends, who show up as a group and form a dense clot around the *kallah* right near the front door, and there's no way to get around them, even though you desperately have to because at 11:30 your babysitter is going to turn into a pumpkin.

- There is the guy who takes the word *l'chaim* literally, and wants everyone around him to drink also. (Ginger ale notwithstanding, I don't know why it's so important for people to actually make a *l'chaim* at a *l'chaim*. It's not like anyone says a *vort* at a *vort*.)

- There is the guy who shows up already smelling like schnapps.

- There is the aunt who spends the entire *simchah* trying to invite the *chassan* and *kallah* over for some random Shabbos in the future, despite the fact that they don't even know when they're getting married yet.

- There are at least five guests who are related to both the *chassan* AND the *kallah*. The Jewish family tree intersects with itself a LOT.

- There is the tired uncle who came straight from work and doesn't say much to anyone and would obviously rather be in bed.

- There's the youngest brother of either the *chassan* or the *kallah*, whom everyone feels they have to ask how it feels to have a sibling who's engaged. I assure you that he doesn't know.
- There is the relative who was told about the engagement about five minutes before the party, and yet has managed to get his name on the engagement gift from the rest of the family.
- There is the aunt who shows up late and brings along half the food, and then tries to make casual conversation while trying to subtly cut open a box of bakery cake with a set of car keys.
- There is the friend of the *chassan* who makes it very obvious that he has not eaten supper yet, even though it is 10:30 at night. "Whoa, is that cantaloupe?"
- And then there's the guy who initiates the dancing. Dancing at a *l'chaim* is very nice, but it's always the same guy.

So I barely got to say a word to the *chassan*. But it's good to have all of these people together, despite their differences in personality (and height), because that is what a *l'chaim* is all about – having friends and family come together to say and do the same things at every *simchah*. But that's just how it is, and that's what makes a family so funny.

We really have to do something about organizing the dancing at weddings. When I went to my sister's *chasunah* recently, I spent most of the time either dancing or posing for pictures, and dancing has not gotten any better since all my friends were getting married.

There's a lot of dancing to be done at weddings, but not a lot of moves. First there's a huge amount of backward dancing, where the entire crowd claps and bounces up and down and surges blindly backward, stepping on toes, running into chairs, fake trees, walls, grandparents, etc. We dance the *chassan* into the *bedekin*, and then we dance him right back out of there, and then we dance him

Dancing Backward

and the *kallah* back up the aisle after the *chuppah*. That's a lot of backward dancing. I suspect that some of these people get into their cars after the wedding and turn on the music and back their cars all the way home.

But it's not all backward dancing. Once the *chassan* and *kallah* are introduced "for the very first time", not including the after-*chuppah* picture fiesta, we have crowded dancing. No matter how many people there are at the wedding, and no matter if the dance floor is the size of Milwaukee, the general custom seems to be that all dancing should take place on an area that is no larger than three feet by three feet. As the dancing goes on, more people keep joining the circle, but it somehow doesn't get any bigger. No one spreads out to accommodate for anything, so you eventually end up squashed between the guy behind you, who is holding your hand in a way that it is awkwardly twisted behind your back, and the guy in front of you, whose back is completely drenched despite the fact that dancing just started thirty seconds ago. How did he get so wet so fast? Was there some kind of accident at the washing station?

So usually you wind up with a slow-moving, densely packed circle, in which not everyone's feet are even necessarily touching the floor, but no one wants to spread out or start a new outer circle, because that would violate the three-feet custom. So instead, they try to make a new circle *within* the outer circle. They figure that this way, there is more of a chance that they will be seen by the *chassan*, who will then dance with them for twenty seconds, and then they can go stand off to the side somewhere with their ginger ale and wait for the next dance to begin.

But then the people in the outer circle decide that the people in the inner circle seem to be having more fun, or at least they're moving faster. Plus, they don't like that everyone in their circle is constantly bumping into the photographer's stepladder, and they're afraid that any minute he's going to fall on somebody. (He won't, by the way. Wedding photographers have great balance. They do this every night. Have you ever seen a wedding photographer walking across the top of a *mechitzah*?) So about two thirds of the outer circle, at the same time, leaves the outer circle and attempts to merge with the inner circle, until the inner circle has more people in it than the outer circle does, and the outer circle snaps. I am routinely in the outer circle when this happens, and I suddenly find myself with no one in front of me, dragging a trail of people behind me by the hand. I hate being the front guy. Where should I take these people? Should I try to go *around* the stepladder instead of *through* it? And then all of a sudden, it's just me and like two other guys, holding hands and dancing around the inner circle, which by now has expanded to contain yet another circle. Then I go sit down for a while.

But at least it's better than being the front of a train. I am referring here to the dance wherein everyone grabs onto each other's shoulders and races around the room, weaving in and out of tables, straight through the dancing circle, out onto the street, etc. (I usually end up behind the guy with the wet back again.) But if you're in the front of a train, everyone follows you. That's a lot of pressure. You can't even shake them off, because they'll think that's part of the dance. "Okay, everyone, shake; he's shaking!" You go out to make a phone call, and there they all are, blindly following you. One Simchas Torah when I was a kid, I found myself in a train that took us to a completely different shul. They had great candy. But I have no idea how to get back there again.

The second dance at weddings is generally a little less crowded, because by then everyone with a babysitter has gone home. So at that point everyone usually dances the Horah, which has real dance steps, which are three steps forward, one step back. (It's kind of like marriage, in a way.) The dance seems pretty simple, but there are always a few people who are one step behind the entire time, still going back when everyone else is trying to go forward, and they're totally oblivious. They don't even notice that they're off. Also, there's always one over-enthusiastic father who brings his three-year-old into the circle, and the poor kid keeps tripping over his own feet and getting jerked back and forth like a rag doll, and everyone else is afraid of stepping on him.

For the Horah, the band plays either *"Asher Bara"* (the Piamenta one – it would be very hard to dance the Horah to the Miami one) or else they play *"Ben Bag Bag"*. Those are the only two Horah songs they play. You can go over and request another song, and they'll say, "Yeah, we know that one!" And then they'll play *"Ben Bag Bag"* again. Which is unfortunate, because no one knows the words.

Also, depending on the family's custom, at some point either the *chassan* or the *chassan* and *kallah* sit down in the middle of the circle, probably to wonder if marriage is always this tiring, and some guys with a complete lack of stage fright go into the middle of the circle to dance in front of them, or to maybe do some things that technically are not considered dancing, such as eating flowers and lighting themselves on fire. And there's always some guy who has to jump rope, using a string of handkerchiefs that he spent the entire *seudah* tying together so that no one within a five-table radius had anything to wipe their faces on.

I have no idea what the women are doing in the meantime. At the end of my sister's *chasunah*, I cut through the women's section to find a bunch of tiny round pieces of paper on the floor. Do they throw confetti at each other? Was there a hole-punching party? Also, sometimes after a wedding I see the *kallah's* friends walking around with some spectacularly random items, such as a six-foot teddy bear, or a bunch of picket signs. What were they protesting? Taxidermy? My wife, however, assures me that there is plenty of pushing and fumbling of dance moves on the women's side also.

So something definitely has to be done about this. Not at the actual weddings, though. No one can hear you over the music anyway. But maybe someone should write some kind of column about it, using ideas he jotted down on the back of his place card, in the hopes of raising awareness.

I'm not talking about me, of course. I'm talking about someone else. I have to do something about all of these guys hanging off the back of my shoulders.

Unabashed

The reason that I ran out to the Syms Bash on a Sunday afternoon was not because everyone I knew was going to be there. The reason I went was because I really, really needed a new suit.

The Syms Bash is not held every day. If Syms had low prices all the time, no one would go to Syms. They'd just look for a *cheaper* place. So Syms lowers its prices twice a year, and everyone mobs the store. Shoprite does the same thing with can-cans. In fact, most of the people who run over to Syms aren't even looking to buy anything – they're just there to mill around and get in the way, and to crowd the semi-private dressing rooms. ("Semi-private" means that there is a curtain in front of the dressing room, but on the inside it's just one big room, so that anyone can take their sweet time walking in and then forget to close the curtain. Also, there are mirrors on the walls.)

I, however, really *did* need a suit. I had only one suit that I knew for sure fit me, plus a bunch of others hanging in my closet that I could never remember either way whether or not they fit. As for the one suit that for sure fit, I had bought it two and a half years earlier at a Syms in Massachusetts about an hour and a half before Yom Tov.

It seems that every second time that my wife and I visit her parents in Massachusetts, we forget our suit bag. The first time we did this was when we went up for our Shabbos *sheva brachos*. My wife rummaged through her old closet and found an emergency back-up outfit she'd never worn before (and never since), but my situation was more of a problem. I am a couple of sizes bigger than my father-in-law, and could not get away with shoehorning myself into one of his suits and walking the half-hour to shul and sitting at *sheva brachos* for three hours while a bunch of people I didn't know whispered to each other about what kind of boy my wife was marrying that wore his bar mitzvah suit to his Shabbos *sheva brachos*. So instead, I ended up wearing my weekday pants, and a borrowed jacket that was so large that I could have wrapped it around myself twice, and I probably should have, because it is COLD in Massachusetts.

So the last time we forgot our Shabbos clothes, which we didn't notice until we unloaded the car about two hours before Yom Tov, we immediately jumped back into the car and hightailed over to Syms. As soon as we got there, we split up, and I ran right over to where they kept the suits – one step up from the rest of the store.

It's nice to know that, even out in the sticks, Syms keeps their suits one step up from the rest of the store. Why do they do this? Are they worried about flooding?

As soon as I got there, it suddenly struck me that I had no idea what size suit I was, but I did know that I was a thirty-eight in pants, so I grabbed a handful of size thirty-eight suits and sprinted for the dressing area, probably leaving a trail of pants and jackets behind me as I ran. I was followed in by a little old man who I would say probably worked there, because he was wearing a tape measure. He looked me up and down, and told me, almost painfully slowly, that I was not a thirty-eight, and then he steered me toward the proper rack. I think it's so cool that he could just look at me and know what size I am. That could be a very useful talent. Like when a policeman asks a witness how tall the suspect was, and the witness thinks to himself, "How am I supposed to know? Should I just wear a tape measure around my neck all the time?" This guy would just look the cop in the eye and say, "He was a forty-two portly." Or you're at the zoo, looking at the cows, and he's clearly thinking, "That one is a seventy-eight husky." We're betting these guys don't have great marriages.

I bought a suit in record time, and then we headed over to the town *shaatnez* checker, who was willing to fit us into her schedule an hour before Yom Tov. This isn't really funny, but I wanted to thank her one more time in a public forum before my suit goes to that big Purim costume box in the sky.

I think that my suit has served its time. I've worn it every Shabbos for about two-and-a-half years, except for that one time I forgot to pack a suit when we went to my *parents'* house, and the seat is so shiny that the kid who stands behind me in shul can straighten his tie in the reflection. I try to wear a different tie every week so that it will look like I'm wearing different suits, but I suspect that anyone who recognizes where all of the stains are already knows.

I found out about the bash on the very last day that it ran, which was a Sunday. I immediately dropped everything I was doing (namely, the weight-gain column that ran last week), and drove out to the store, where I ended up running into everyone I knew, and comparing notes:

"Hey, what are you doing in the 'PORTLY' section?"

"What are *you* doing in the 'ATHLETIC' section?"

(We all bumped into each other again later at the *Shaatnez* Center: "What are you doing at the *Shaatnez* Center?" [Syms Bash week is like tax season for the *shaatnez* community.])

I spent about three hours trying on suits until I felt that I had tried on every suit in the Western Hemisphere. My problem was that, for every suit that I tried on that the jacket fit okay, the pants were too tight, and for every suit that the pants fit, the jacket sleeves were too short. Apparently, I'm built like a chimp. So I tried going over to one of the sales reps to see if they could tell me, just by looking, what size I was. (It's almost like the guy at the carnival who guesses your weight. You're almost tempted to approach him wearing lifts and holding in your stomach, but then *nobody* wins.) As it was, one rep said I was a 44 regular, which I knew, after trying on all of the 44 regulars, that I clearly was *not*, and the other rep said I was portly. At some point I wanted to mix and match to make myself a suit that actually fit, but apparently you're not allowed to do that, although, after trying on some of those suits, I was wondering if people didn't already secretly mix and match in the semi-private dressing room and then casually put their leftovers back on the rack on the way out.

In the end, I walked out with two suits, in case my wife didn't like one of them. My wife generally doesn't like me in double-breasted suits, because they make me look like I'm hiding something, and my mother has never liked me in three-button suits, because they make me look like a hot dog. So I got one of each. I'm planning on switching off wearing them every other week, and maybe just always wearing the same tie.

Running With Scissors

Being a parent isn't easy. It's not just about making sure your kids don't run around the house with scissors; we have to make sure they grow into responsible adults who are capable of raising their *own* kids into responsible adults. And it's not like your first kid comes along with a little manual, nor is there a license exam that we have to take, before which we can only be a parent if we have an experienced parent sitting right next to us and hanging onto the overhead strap for dear life. All we have are the memories of how our parents raised us, and of how, at the time, we never missed the opportunity to tell them what a horrible job they were doing. And then there's the knowledge that if we make a mistake, there's no way we can go back and fix it. So essentially, we, as parents, are all running with scissors.

Now it's time for: "Road Trip Advice for People Who Don't Know Better," the only Question and Answer advice column to have been officially recognized by the American Automobile Association of America as being a bad idea to begin with. This column features well-meaning advice to actual questions on car travel sent in by actual readers who don't actually exist. And so, without further ado, we shall begin:

Q: Why do families go on long car trips during the summer?

A: There are many different reasons why people decide to subject themselves to long summer drives. Some of them may be tired of the hot, stuffy city environment in which they live, and would feel more comfortable driving long distances with the windows rolled down while waiting for the air conditioner to stop blowing hot air, and fighting radio static. These people hope to eventually get to their bungalow colonies, where the air is thinner and the pool freezes over in the middle of the night.

Q: Why don't they just move into the bungalows for good?

A: They're not too crazy about living in 1700s-style huts, either.

Q: Are there any other reasons why people may want to drive long distances?

A: Some people may want to visit popular tourist attractions featuring friendly people with enormously misshapen heads, such as Disney World or one of the square states. Their goal is to spend as much money as they can to be able to wait on line.

Q: So why don't they just go by plane?

A: Not *that* much money.

Q: I have a job in middle management, in which my duties include walking around with a coffee mug and bugging people for coming in late. Over the last few years, I have racked up an enormous amount of unused sick days, to the point where I can get marooned on a desert island and no one will know the difference. My question is this: Do you think it's something in the coffee?

Road Trip Advice for People Who Don't Know Better

A: It would not surprise us one bit.

Q: Do you think I need a vacation?

A: From the coffee? Yes. We think you should drop whatever you're doing, especially if it's important, load up the family car, and hit the road.

Q: What about the children?

A: If you plan on taking the children, you're going to have to do a lot more in the way of packing. You will not be able to get away with the same two pairs of socks and a toothbrush that suffice when it's just you and your spouse. With kids, you have to bear in mind that they will need a complete set of summer clothes, a set of winter clothes, a raincoat for the water rides, games for when they get bored, more games for when they get bored of the games, snacks for when they're hungry, snacks for when they're not really hungry but just saw other kids eating snacks, and a huge box with the word "miscellaneous" spelled wrong in magic marker. And if your plan is to sneak your kids out of camp on visiting day, you're also going to have to leave room in your vehicle for their sleeping bags, their pillows, and their impossibly big bags of dirty laundry.

Q: Whoa.

A: Yes.

Q: How are we supposed to carry it all?

A: One way to move around excess luggage is to tie it down to the roof of your car, while taking great care not to accidentally tie your car doors shut. You can also purchase one of those

A CLEVER TITLE GOES HERE

big plastic turtle shells to attach to your luggage rack and then spend most of your vacation driving slowly through tollbooths and tunnels because you're not really sure how tall your car is with the shell. Also, while driving along the highway, you will notice that some people handle the luggage problem by dragging their luggage behind them via trailers, motor homes, motorboats, All-Terrain-Vehicle carriers, and bicycle racks. This allows them to potentially block six or seven lanes of traffic while trying to make an exit.

Q: What about minivans or station wagons?

A: Many people nowadays like to use minivans, because most station wagons were manufactured back when people had to pull into gas stations and make it a point to ask for unleaded gas. On the other hand, station wagons are generally cheaper, due to the fact that some of the seats were put in backwards. Many children like them, too, because it's easier for them to kick each other.

Q: How about sport utility vehicles?

A: These are actually the best, because they allow you to drive over other cars in traffic situations.

Q: How can I stop my children from fighting in the backseat?

A: That is an excellent question, and I'm glad I made it up. The truth is that children will *always* fight in the backseat. It is part of growing up. Back when the Jews were travelling through the

Road Trip Advice for People Who Don't Know Better

desert, parents were often heard telling their children, "If you guys don't stop fighting back there, I'm going to turn this cart around, and we are GOING BACK TO EGYPT!" This kind of threat rarely works nowadays, because children know full well that their parents are not about to show their faces back at work when they're supposed to be spending the week in Cape Cod. Their co-workers would ask them right away, "Hey, I thought you were on vacation. What happened?" "Well, we got about halfway there, but then the kids started spitting at each other. Maybe next year." Instead, you're going to have to exercise parental threats that your kids know you will follow through on, such as, "If you don't stop pulling your sister's hair, then Mommy's going to be angry."

Q: I'm on vacation, so I can't be bothered to come up with creative threats for my children. Do you have any other ideas?

A: Well, you can always take the approach that was first implemented a short while ago by millionaire philanthropist Dennis Tito. What Dennis did was he paid the Russians millions of dollars to take him up into outer space.

Q: What did the Russians do with the money?

A: They sent it to Siberia, where it froze to death.

Q: So what did he do up there in space?

A: Well, the Russians, who realized his significance as the world's first space tourist ever, kept him locked in a little section of the space station and posted a bunch of signs prohibiting flash photography. If he wanted to visit any other part of the spaceship, he needed an escort. Also, if he broke something, he would have to contribute millions more dollars to the Russians.

Q: It sounds sort of like a prison.

A: You should have seen the food. It was all the same consistency and came out of toothpaste tubes.

Q: So why would I want to go up to space?

A: Well, for one thing, you wouldn't have to exercise any parental threats, except on the Russians. You wouldn't have to stop anywhere for directions, either, unless you would forget which way was up. And lastly, you wouldn't have to pay for hotels or anything. You'd just stay in the spaceship.

Q: But isn't that like loading up the car, driving it around, and then parking it right back in your driveway?

A: Yes.

Q: Hmm.

A: So you'd rather stick with your kids?

Q: I'd rather stick with my kids.

The first and only time that I went to sleep-away camp, my parents urged me to write home at least twice a week. I am an oldest child, and they had a hard time letting go. This is as opposed to nowadays, when they're never quite sure which of their kids are in the house at any given moment. They get a letter in the mail, and they're like, "Moishe's at camp?!"

My grandparents, meanwhile, wanted me to write them at least once a week, which I guess was okay. People should write their grandparents once in a while, even if they actually live with them, because grandparents save every letter they get in a small keepsake box that smells like mothballs. But then two of my aunts called me before camp specifically to remind me to write to them once a week, which I thought was strange, because if I'd been home, chances were I would not have communicated with them *at all* over the summer. And another aunt told me I should write to her son in camp, because she could not for the life of her get him to sit down and write letters, and she thought I would set an example. As if ten-year-old boys look at letters from their cousins and go: "Huh. An example." And I had to write to my great-grandmother, everyone kept reminding me. Also, my two youngest aunts, one of them two years older than me, and the other four, told me that they were going to send me letters, and that I had better write back. But I had no intention of writing them, and I actually dreaded getting those letters, from two girls with different last names from mine, care of Camp Bnos. It was like the eyes of the entire camp were on me.

So I spent most of the summer writing letters. The camp did give us time to write letters – about a half-hour twice a week, and I could not imagine how all of those kids fit so many letters into such a small time frame. And that was besides for the fact that, as a creative child, I felt that every letter I wrote had to be different. I couldn't send two people the same letter. What if they read each other's mail? Then they'd know it wasn't personalized. (I now find that this rule also holds true in writing cover letters to go with your resumes.)

I mainly wrote these letters on the sidelines while the rest of my bunk played sports. I was not what you'd call athletic; I was more the type of kid who never played sports because I wasn't good at it, and wasn't good at it because I never played sports. I'd apparently missed the part of childhood where everyone came out onto the field and said, "Okay, we're all horrible at this; let's get better together." By the time I showed up, everyone already knew how to hit a baseball and play kickball in such a way that they did not miss the ball and fall over. I was more the type of kid who stood way out in left field and thought about candy and spent the entire game *davening* that the ball wouldn't come near me.

But I did have a good time at camp, though. I enjoyed most of the activities that didn't involve any amount of athletic ability, such as "Capture the Counselor", when all of the campers went out at night with flashlights to look for the counselors, whom I'm pretty sure spent most of the night at the pizza shop, because no one found any of them for a really long time, and then they turned up in places that we knew for certain we'd already checked. I also enjoyed Color War, except for the part where each team gets points based on how loud the kids *daven* when the head counselor comes near them. It always gave me a headache, and the way I understood it, Hashem doesn't care if you daven *loud*; Hashem cares if you daven *well*. So apparently everyone was *davening* to the head counselor, which was kind of pointless, because in the end he made it a tie.

But the part of camp to which I most looked forward was definitely visiting day. On visiting day, I didn't have to play sports or write letters. Instead, I got to give my parents a grand tour of the camp. I showed them my bunkhouse, which smelled like feet and consisted of thin, flimsy mattresses perched over impossibly huge bags of dirty laundry; I showed them the infirmary, of which I had never seen the inside (because I never played sports) except for the day *after* visiting day, when the camp decided to break out Color War by having a fake health inspector show up and insist that everyone get tested for lead poisoning; and I got to show them the lake, where the dock had collapsed the week before while all of the campers were in bed, and everyone had thought it was part of some elaborate Color War breakout scheme, and all of the counselors denied knowing what happened.

I even introduced my father to the counselor, who had a long conversation with him that ended in my father giving him a handshake full of money. It turns out that counselors look forward to visiting day also, and they spend the entire morning running around and cleaning up while the campers are sitting in the lunchroom and listening to the head counselor drone on about the rules of visiting day, such as not to run off with anyone else's parents, and not to mention the kid who ended up in the hospital. The counselors want to present a clean house in an attempt to convince the parents that they are attending to the children's every need, rather than burying their heads under their pillows and wondering why they ended up with a bunk that had so much energy at six in the morning. They'd sweep the bunkhouses, fix the hinges on the doors, lure out the small woodland creature from beneath the floorboards (or shovel them out, as the case may be), scrub the letters off each child's bar of soap to make it look used, spray half of each can of deodorant in the direction of the woodland creatures, and squirt out half of each tube of toothpaste. If they are thorough enough, it may result in a nice-sized tip; if they are not, they can be expected to have some confused mothers asking them how their son came to use up half of a tube of toothpaste if the toothbrush is still in the package.

But soon my parents left, and I had to go back to writing them letters. And for some reason, all of the outgoing mail got held up, so I spent two whole weeks writing letters, and then reading about how I wasn't writing letters. My parents then got them all a few days after

I got home. "Hey, look!" they announced excitedly. "You sent us a letter!" Turns out, it was all stuff that I'd told them already.

The problem with putting our kids to bed early is that by the time we finally get them to lie down, we're more tired than they are. Nevertheless, we tell ourselves that we're doing this so that our kids can get the proper amount of sleep as recommended by the experts, who were out studying to become experts while their spouses were spending their evenings chasing their kids around with a pajama top. Meanwhile, our kids don't fall asleep until about an hour after their bedtimes, and then they're bouncing around their rooms again at six in the morning.

No; the real reason that we put our kids to bed early is so that we can actually get things done, like writing articles and doing laundry,

Time to Think

and that parents in general need a certain amount of peace and quiet every day to keep their sanity. That's why once you hit your teenage years and started going to bed later than your parents, your parents developed a permanent glazed look and started forgetting things and began verbally going through the names of all of their kids every time they wanted to get your attention. ("Alright, Av... Sar...Yitz...Rivk...What *is* your name?")

So we need to get our kids to bed on time. The problem is that kids don't *want* to go to bed on time. They can't stand the thought that they're lying in bed, and you're having the time of your life downstairs, balancing checkbooks and washing dishes. So they creep out of bed to see what's going on, like they think they're invisible, and when they realize that you can in fact see them, they come up with the first excuse they can think of:

"Can you tuck me in?" ("I *did* tuck you in. You got up.")

"I need a drink of water." ("You don't even *like* water.")

"There's a monster under my bed." ("Good. Maybe he'll do some cleaning.")

When I was a kid, I rarely got out of bed at night. But that didn't mean that I went right to sleep either. On most nights, I would read books by the tiny crack of light coming in from the door. And then every year before Pesach I would rearrange all of my furniture so that my bed was in a better position to receive light from the door, until the one year that I pretty much put my bed smack in the middle of the room, and my mother complained because she couldn't get to my brother's crib.

Another thing that I used to do in bed was get dressed. It took me forever to get dressed in the morning, because I loved to space out. There's nothing like sitting at the edge of your bed, with your shirt unbuttoned and only one sock on, dreaming about nothing. My parents had a big problem with this, because they had to keep poking their heads into my room and reminding me to get dressed.

"Get dressed," they'd say.

"Okay," I'd say, and I'd put on my other sock and close maybe two buttons, and then go back to spacing out. (I'm actually surprised that I turned out as well as I did.) So at one point, I figured that it would take me less time to get dressed in the morning if I had already put on all of my clothes the night before, and all I would have to do in the morning was put on my shoes, and I'd be done. But what if my parents poked their heads in to check on me in the middle of the night? So I put on my pajamas on top of my clothes. I'm pretty sure that my mother was wondering at some point how come all of my pajamas were stretched out.

But I blame all of this on my early bedtime. I am the oldest of ten children, and my parents were determined to start off with rules. But they've definitely gone lax with my later siblings. Right now my youngest brother is nine, and I don't think he even *has* a bedtime. I think he goes from Shabbos to Shabbos.

Another problem with putting a child to bed before he or she is technically tired is that the child suddenly has time to think. And when a child gets to think, he comes up with twenty-five things to say to you that have absolutely no relevance to anything, but that cannot wait until morning. And he comes up with them one at a time. My daughter, Adina, is very good at this.

Time to Think

"Mommy," she says, suddenly appearing from behind a huge pile of laundry. "Why did Grandpa die?" (Grandpa was my wife's grandfather, and passed away last year at age ninety-five.)

"Because he was old," my wife says, having had this conversation a million times. "Now go to bed."

Adina thinks for a second. "*You're* old," she says to my wife.

"No, I'm not," my wife says. "Now go to bed."

"I'm four years old," Adina says.

"I know," my wife says. "Go to bed!"

"My birthday is on Chanukah," Adina says.

"Bed!" my wife says.

"Grandpa had a lot of *menorahs*," Adina says.

My son Daniel takes a different approach. He basically plays loudly at the top of the stairs, and then when he hears us coming, he drops whatever he's holding and leaps into his bed, which is no small feat, because he has the top bunk. I'm thinking that parents should try the same technique when their kids get out of bed. As soon as we hear them coming to ask for a drink or how come cows moo or whatever, we should drop what we're doing and pretend to be asleep. We don't even have to take a flying leap into our beds. We could just do that thing that kids sometimes do, where they lie down in whatever spot they happened to be standing when they got tired. ("Tatty, how come you're sleeping on the floor with a light bulb?")

But I am not an expert. What experts recommend is that you get your kids used to a bedtime routine, during which they know what to expect, and are therefore less likely to disrupt it. For instance, you can have them brush their teeth and say Shema, and then you can read them one of those short bedtime stories, like "Shmonkey Goes to Bed," or "Kalman the Clown Goes to the Therapist," which are written by people who very obviously get paid by the page:

PAGE 1. Kalman the Clown was sad.

PAGE 2. He was very sad.

PAGE 3. He was sad, sad, sad.

PAGE 4. He went to see his friend, Shalom the Shrink.

PAGE 5. "Why are you sad?" asked Shalom.

PAGE 6. "I will tell you why I am sad," said Kalman. "But not on this page."

PAGE 7. "Don't be sad," said Shalom.

PAGE 8. "Oh," said Kalman. "Okay."

PAGE 9. "Hurray!" said Shalom. "That'll be five hundred dollars."

Of course, the main danger with a story like this is that it will give your kids even more things to think about. ("Mommy, what's a shrink?")

Other experts recommend that you give your kids things to think about that *won't* draw them out of bed. Like you could tell them about something exciting that they're going to do tomorrow, or you could ask them about their favorite thing that happened today, or you can give them a difficult math problem: "There is a train heading west from Boston at sixty miles per hour, and another train heading south…"

Anyway, that's it for now. I'm going to bed.

Shmoozing About Snoozing

People love to sleep. Ever since the dawn of civilization, mankind has pretty much resolved never to be awake for another dawn if they could help it. Even during *Makkas Bechoros*, with half of Egypt dying around him, Pharaoh did not get out of bed until the absolute last second, and had to run around town in his pajamas in the middle of the night.

But even nowadays, we are not much different. Let's look at the typical morning of Yoni Q. Publicstein, who has a family, a mortgage, and a nine-to-five job that requires him to wear a tie. In general, his mornings go something like this:

5:30 A.M. – Alarm goes off

A CLEVER TITLE GOES HERE

5:39 A.M. – Alarm goes off

5:48 A.M., 5:57 A.M., 6:06 A.M. -- Alarm goes off

6:15 A.M. – Alarm goes off

6:16 A.M. – Yoni comes up with a basic plan of what he's going to do that day. It pretty much involves going to work and coming home.

6:24 A.M. – Alarm goes off

6:26 A.M. – Nods off in a standing position on the way to the bathroom

6:30 A.M. – Falls asleep on the edge of the bathtub with his toothbrush dangling out of his mouth

6:33 A.M. – Alarm goes off

6:34 A.M. – Takes a shower to try to wake himself up

6:44 A.M. – Realizes that he just spent a full ten minutes washing his neck

6:46 A.M. – Gets out of the shower and goes back to the bedroom. He turns on the light so that he can find that suit that he likes without the *cholent* stains.

6:47 A.M. – Wife turns off the light

7:00 A.M. – Yoni wakes up in the kitchen with his pants on backward

7:01 A.M. – He puts up a pot of coffee

7:07 A.M. – Yoni and his wife sit, quietly sipping their coffee. Yoni drinks his coffee black, with no milk, no sugar, and no water. Just heated coffee crystals. His wife uses decaf crystals.

Shmoozing About Snoozing

7:15 A.M. – Yoni, his briefcase and *tallis* bag in hand, finally gets out of the house. As he rounds the corner, a thought hits the back of his mind: "Hey, didn't we have kids?"

7:16 A.M. – Alarm goes off

Yoni's situation is not unique. Many people have trouble getting out of bed. Of course, they're not always like that. Most people start off as babies, who have no problem whatsoever waking up in the middle of the night, primarily to get back at their parents for making them go to sleep five times during the day. Their parents grudgingly get up, because otherwise the babies will cry straight until the next feeding time, and then what are the parents going to do? Feed the babies twice? And the babies don't have built-in snooze buttons to keep them quiet for nine-minute stretches – they just have that soft spot in the middle of their heads. This is what's known in the computer industry as "room for expansion".

After a while, these babies get older and mutate into children, who are just like adults, but with larger vocal cords. Children are quick to jump out of bed in the morning, so that they can make loud, unexplained noises and jump down all of the stairs at once and eat an entire box of a high-energy cereal that has its name spelled wrong for legal reasons and makes its milk glow in the dark. And then the kids bound back to their parents' bedroom, so that they can bounce on their parents' beds, which still contain their actual parents, while the parents themselves bury their heads under their pillows and try to fall back asleep and have unusually vivid dreams about stampeding livestock.

But then, at some point during the child's development, he or she begins to notice that so long as he or she is asleep, he or she

A CLEVER TITLE GOES HERE

is not, for the moment, sitting in a hard chair and trying to figure out how many trains travel from New York to Boston and back, and how fast they're going to meet, and at what point they're going to realize that they're traveling on the same track. And so he or she resorts to staying awake for most of the night, raiding the fridge, and then sleeping for as many daylight hours as possible, and of course have dreams about being in school anyway. But that is why teenagers usually look like they've just woken up.

This system works pretty well for a while, barring the occasional annoying parent trying to wake them up before it is technically noon for some lame reason such as that they've fallen asleep in their cereal. But at some point most of them are going to grow up and join the work force, and they're going to notice that what was once the solution has now become the problem. You *want* to get up; you *have* to get up; you in fact set several alarms to wake you up, yet when morning comes you lie there with your eyes closed and decide that you don't actually *need* to get up, because even if you lose your job and have to sell your house and your car, you can always keep your bed. But this isn't *you* talking; this is your "morning person", who looks pretty much like you except that he has no facial features and bad breath. And in fact, your morning person has actually trained himself to get out of bed and unplug the alarm clock *without actually waking up*.

In fact, what you are beginning to suspect – and you strongly believe that the scientific community should stop messing around with diseases and start looking into this – is that your bed is situated over a powerful gravity well that doesn't let you get up in the morning and also drags your shoes under the bed and messes with the A.M. / P.M. settings on your clock.

Thankfully, at least someone in the scientific community has their priorities straight. I am referring here to the researchers at Nanda, Inc., who invented "Clocky" – an alarm clock that, as soon as you hit the snooze button, actually rolls off your nightstand and across the room and hides, so that nine minutes later you have to get out of bed and play hot and cold with an annoying little alarm clock. (In 2005, Nanda won an Ig Nobel Prize for their invention.) Clocky is designed on the principal that, once you actually find it, assuming you don't smash it with a hammer, you are going to be awake enough that you may as well start your day. It is also a great deterrent for keeping empty drinking glasses on the night table.

But maybe "Clocky" is actually on to something with all of the hiding and the seeking. Maybe the key is to actually convince your "morning person" that you are still a kid, and therefore have to get up really early and put your shirt on backward and eat "Frooty-Klumps" until you are no longer sure which way is up. Convincing your morning person of this should not be too difficult, considering how tired and incoherent he or she is likely to be. All it would take is a few simple changes: a pair of footsy pajamas festooned with pictures of animals wearing pants, some randomly-placed stuffed animals (the teddy bear kind, not the taxidermy kind), and, if your parents live close by, driving over to their place and bouncing on the beds until *they* wake up. But the truth is that they might not even be in bed anymore, because the elderly tend to wake up early. Maybe we should find out how *they* do it.

I don't know if I'm going to get anyone into trouble for saying this, but parents don't like when their children have off from school. Sure, you liked it when *you* were a kid, and your parents seemingly had nothing to do with their time other than wait eagerly for you to come home from school so they could take care of you.

But now that you're a parent, a day off from school means that you're stuck trying to figure out what to do with your kids. Because it turns out that you don't actually have off on most of those days. Chances are, your boss doesn't give you midwinter vacation and two months off during the summer and three random days of Chanukah and Shushan Purim. So you have to go to work.

Caution: Kids At Work

So seemingly, the only solution, if you want those days off also, is to become a teacher. This is a pretty good idea, except that:

- No two schools ever give exactly the same days off. All of the schools in the world coordinate this via extensive five-thousand-way conference calls, so that even if you have one kid in the school near you, one kid in the school across town, one in Lakewood, one in Cleveland, and one in Switzerland, every single child will have different vacation days. It's amazing how they do this. For Chanukah vacation alone, one of your children will have Friday and Sunday off, one will have Thursday and Friday, one will have Sunday and Monday, one will have Wednesday and the following Wednesday, and one will have off on all eight days from noon until two fifteen. They even do this with different grades in the same school. So even if you're a teacher, there's no way you're going to have the same days off as *all* of your kids, unless you pressure your younger kids to succeed in school, and your older kids to do poorly, so that they all end up in the same grade. But even so,

- Most teachers don't make enough money to have only one job. Apparently, all that tuition doesn't go to the teachers. It goes to the expensive conference calls, and to the non-teacher personnel, such as the janitor, who apparently spends most of it on ammonia. With all that ammonia they're inhaling, no wonder our kids are doing so poorly on standardized tests. That, and the fact that they have too many days off.

Another problem is snow days. Most major corporations do not give off for snow days. So while our kids love them, we adults have to waste our vacation days on them, so that we have to go to work on Chol Hamoed and Erev Yom Kippur and Erev Pesach, so that we can spend these snow days wiping noses and telling our kids to stop trekking snow through the house and trying to explain to them why they can't go sledding down the slope of the front lawn into parked cars. So sometimes you just have to bring your kids to work.

I myself sometimes bring kids to work (usually my own), because I have a very nice boss who understands what it's like to be a parent, and also pretends not to notice when I work on humor columns on company time. Yes, I know that I have previously mentioned that I am a teacher, plus I write humor articles, which my editors then turn into slightly shorter humor articles. But it turns out that writing humor columns pays just enough that I have to get *three* jobs to make ends meet.

So by day I work for a company that sells appliances over the phone and online to people who have figured out that if they actually go into the *store* to buy a fridge, which their wife has insisted has to have the largest capacity available, then they might have to personally drag it outside to the car and strap it to the roof and drive slowly and brake very carefully and somehow figure out how to get it into the house when it is much, much bigger than the front door. Or maybe they'll just leave it out in the yard, and run an extension cord, or build a new house around it. And besides, who is going to get rid of the old refrigerator? And who is going to install the icemaker? Does the wife think that it will just start making ice as soon as the unit is plugged in? Where is the water going to come from? The electrical outlet? So they order their appliances from us, and we get it into their homes and in working order via magic. I'm not too sure about the specifics, because that's not really my end of the business. My end of the business is sitting in the office and yelling at the printer. But I'm a little more careful about the yelling when I bring my kids in.

My kids are usually pretty good when I bring them to work, because I always try to be ready for them. For instance, I always keep some toys in my top desk drawer, and they always spend at least three minutes on the toys before they go straight for the drawer where I keep my nosh. I have a nosh drawer, because my other main function, over at the office, is to slowly eat my weight in chocolate. So my kids usually want to spend the entire seven hours eating. But they never want the oatmeal. I'm starting to wonder why I even *have* oatmeal.

Also, sometimes I print out coloring pages so that my kids can color them with ballpoint pens, because I never do remember to buy crayons. It takes forever to color an entire picture blue with a pen. And sometimes they just occupy themselves with the office supplies, such as use the rubber bands, binder clips, and staples. One time my daughter covered an entire desk in Post-it notes, and on each one she had drawn a little smiley face.

One of my coworkers, Yaakov, occasionally brings his kids in, too, but he doesn't always bring in something for them to do. On Chanukah he brought in his eight-year-old son, Avi, and his four-year-old son, Ilan, and they mainly entertained themselves by fighting. Eventually, he gave them his cell phone to play with. But what is an eight-year-old boy going to do with a cell phone? So he decided to call the only person he knew whose number was in the phone: his Ima. I'm sure that Ima was thrilled that Abba took two of the kids to work so that she could spend most of the day on the phone with them, trying to make conversation. Avi kept calling her, because he felt cool using a cell phone, but it turned out he had nothing to talk about. This was confirmed by the fact that, every few seconds, he said that word into the phone: "Nothing." In the meantime, Ilan spent the entire time yelling into Avi's other ear: "I wanna talk! I wanna talk!" But Avi wouldn't let him talk. He was too busy saying, "Nothing... Quiet, Ilan, I can't hear!... Nothing."

Finally, he put Ilan on the phone. "Hi, Ima," Ilan said. "Can we go to the park? Abba said no."

This process was repeated throughout the day, until finally, Yaakov said, "If you guys don't behave, I'm going to take you home."

That's an ineffective threat if I ever heard one.

But for some reason, they didn't want to go home.

"Nooo!" they yelled. "We wanna stay here with youuuu!"

I guess that's something to think about.

Tuition Break

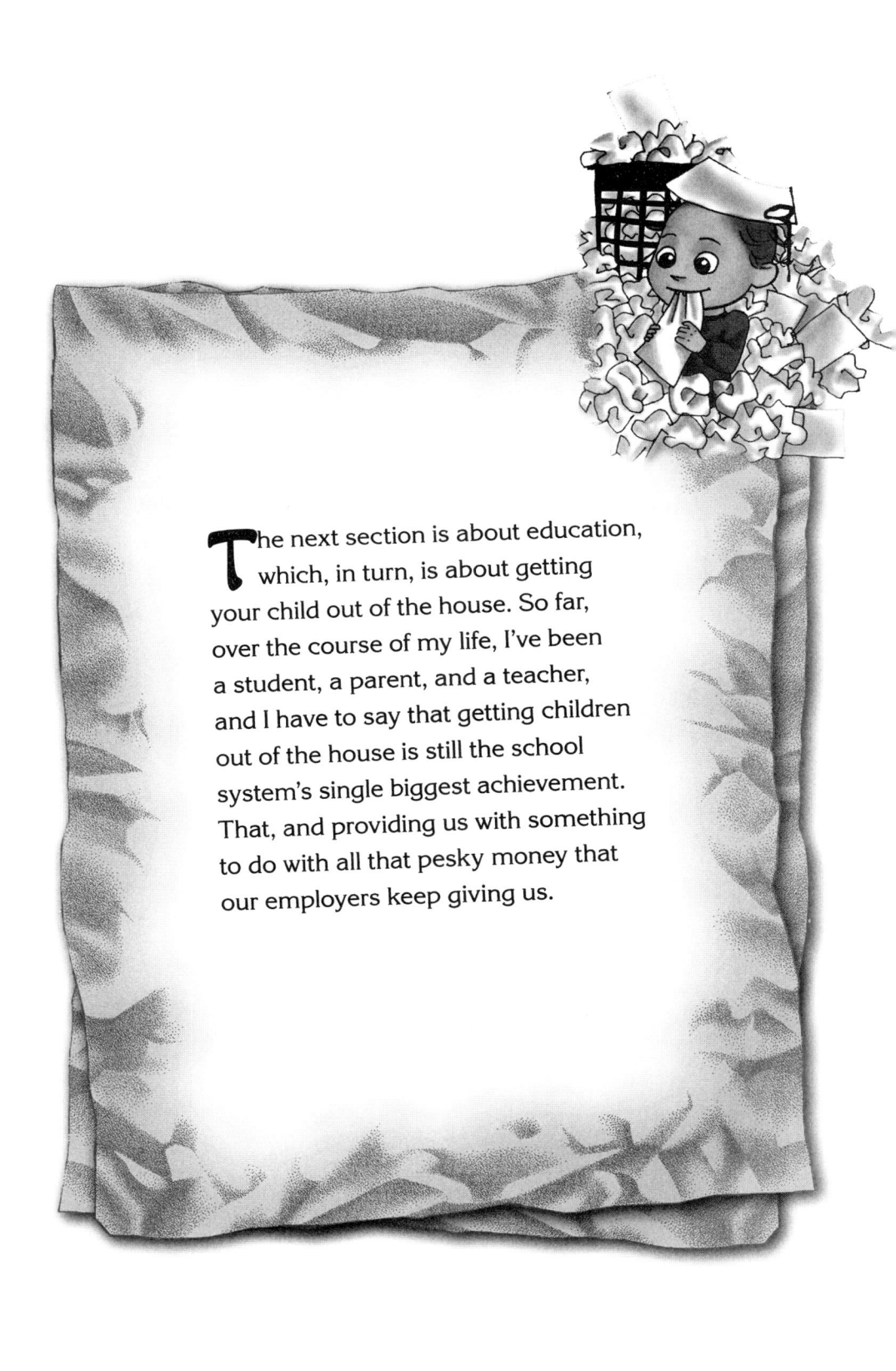

The next section is about education, which, in turn, is about getting your child out of the house. So far, over the course of my life, I've been a student, a parent, and a teacher, and I have to say that getting children out of the house is still the school system's single biggest achievement. That, and providing us with something to do with all that pesky money that our employers keep giving us.

As soon as the summer is just about over, it's finally time to start thinking about sending your kids back to school. Even if school technically doesn't start for another couple of days, don't let that stop you – just usher the little *zeeskeits* out the door and lock it. It's been a long summer, and you can use some peace and quiet.

Of course, you can't even think about sending your children off to school until you stuff their knapsacks with enough office supplies to support a major corporation through several mergers, an indictment, and various employees making use of the printer for their shul newsletters. Most schools will have sent you a helpful reminder list of all of the supplies your children will need on their very first day, despite the fact that the teacher will spend most of that very first day trying to figure out which names go with which faces, and waiting for the office lackey to deliver the textbooks. Nevertheless, you get a list, which reads sort of like a recipe for a huge mess: 1 pair of scissors, 1 pack of loose-leaf paper, 4 glue sticks, etc.

Four glue sticks? On the first day? These kids will be coming home every night, you know!

You can always tell what kind of teachers your children are going to have by what they put on their supplies list. If the teacher wants a box of Crayola eight-count crayons, a box of RoseArt ten-count colored pencils (pre-sharpened), and two boxes of tissues (one for the child's desk, and one for the locker), and then, at the end of the list, the teacher finds it necessary to write "one supply box", then your child is almost certainly going to be coming home with mountains of homework every night. Your more relaxed teachers are a little bit less specific about what to bring. They write things like: "one package loose-leaf paper" or "sneakers". And if the teacher has the kids bring in a yellow highlighter, you know it's her first year teaching.

Much of the time, you can tell that the teachers aren't communicating with each other. When I was in seventh grade, my science teacher requested that we bring in a five-subject notebook, so that we could devote one subject to him. That seemed fair enough. But my social studies teacher wanted us to bring in a single subject notebook, so that we wouldn't confuse it with any of our other subjects. My English teacher (meaning that she *taught* English; I don't think that she *was* English) wanted us to bring in a loose-leaf, so that we could have separate sections for reading, grammar, spelling, vocabulary, writing, and misc. We spent the

Supplies!

entire year of her class playing with those silly little reinforcement rings. My math teacher, meanwhile, *did* want us to bring in a five-subject notebook, but only so that we could rip out the dividers and use the entire book for math. And my *rebbi* insisted on a separate loose-leaf, of course, so that there would be sections for Gemara, *Chumash*, Mishnayos, and *Navi*, although most of us just kept our loose-leafs in our lockers and tucked our loose notes into our Gemara, *Chumash*, and Mishnayos, and we never did end up using our *Navi*. In addition, each of the teachers insisted that we bring in a separate homework pad. There are few things more counterproductive than having to carry around five little homework pads.

There are some items that teachers will always ask for, whether the students will ever actually need them or not. Some teachers will always ask for pencil-topper erasers, in case your child's eraser runs out before his pencil does, which you are well aware, if you've ever seen a child operate an electric pencil sharpener, will never be an issue. And they always insist on Number 2 pencils, to the extent that I am not even sure that any other kind of pencil exists, although my wife assures me that they do, and she's in kitchen design. Also, many teachers will want your child to bring in a compass and a protractor. A compass is a small metal device with a golf pencil that is always falling out and a serious point at the other end that students use to carve fairly obvious statements into desks. A protractor is a piece of plastic that comes with the compass. The purpose of the compass is to teach students how to make circles, although in the real world most of us use a drinking glass. No one has ever made cookies with a compass. Protractors are used for making angles, although no one really knows what to do with the angles once you make them. (My wife assures me that this is not true either.)

Some teachers don't know when to stop, though. My third-grade teacher, Mrs. Berman, had us bring in those black-and-white composition notebooks, and told us that those would be our journals, and that we should write in them every day before she came in. Looking back, I guess that was her way of saying, "I plan to never be here on time, you guys." We wrote in it for maybe two days. As eight-year-old boys, we had better things to do with our time than sit around pretending we had feelings. Another teacher I know of insisted that each child bring in a red folder, a blue folder, and a yellow folder. That way, instead of saying, "Take out your math folder," she could say, "Take out your yellow folder." So some teachers really deserve what they get.

The whole school system is nothing like the real world. In real life, if you don't have what you need, you make do with something else. All of us have at some point used a tissue box to make straight lines, or written down something important with a yellow highlighter. Life is all about learning to make do. But if a teacher writes that your child has to bring in a glue stick, a ruler, and a ream of paper, there is no way you could rummage through your junk drawer and send in a tube of superglue, a tape measure, and a pad with "Motel 6" written in big letters across the top. The teacher doesn't care what you think. She is making barely enough money to pay for the gas to get to school, and she doesn't care if running around town to find a pencil case is cutting into your busy schedule of dumping your kids on her to go off and make a decent salary and not once be expected to wipe anyone's nose.

Supplies!

But that is how it works; no one is happy. The teachers aren't happy because they're wondering how come they are making less than a babysitter, who gets paid per child and does not have to get them to sit down and recite their multiplication tables. The parents aren't happy because they're wondering, based on the amount of tuition that they have to shell out every year, how it is possible that the teachers aren't making enough money to be able to spring for these school supplies themselves. And the school administrators aren't happy because people keep coming up to them on the street and asking them these kinds of questions. But what is the alternative? Pulling your kids out and home-schooling them with your superglue, your tape measure, and your motel stationary? Only if you want everything in the house underlined in yellow highlighter.

Living in the Projects

I think it's about time that we (meaning my wife and I, although if you want to be included, our door is open) figure out what to do with all of our daughter's arts and crafts projects. Not that we have anything against her projects per se. When Adina made her first drawing at thirteen months, probably by accident, my wife and I made a huge deal about it and posted it on the refrigerator, and forced our guests to stare at it until they came up with something to say that was similar to what critics are always spouting at art museums. (Usually: "What am I looking at, exactly?")

But now Adina is in preschool, and is totally obsessed with making projects. My wife and I don't say anything about it, because

Living in the Projects

we want her to develop her creativity so that she can sit around the house like her father and pretend to work. Right now, our fridge is entirely covered in projects, to the point that I am no longer entirely sure that we even *have* a fridge. I suspect that all of our food is being insulated by layers of construction paper.

(On that note, why do they even call it construction paper? Does anyone actually use it in construction? "Hey, Yankel, what's your house made of?" "Construction paper.")

These days, the projects just keep coming. Adina's teachers (whose names I will not mention, but it's definitely safe to assume that at least one of them is named "Morah Rivky", because studies show that over ninety percent of preschool *morahs* are named Rivky) do a project with the children every day, plus they let the children choose what they want to do during playtime, and Adina usually chooses to color, plus we routinely leave her in an aftercare program, where the teachers have the kids make another project, and then when Adina comes home, she usually wants to do *another* project, which is just fine with my wife, because it means that she can make supper without being bothered, and every Tuesday my wife takes the little ones to the local crafts store, where the staff for some reason makes free projects with the kids. (Tuesdays are slow days at crafts stores.) So on the average week, we're talking about approximately fifteen to twenty projects, all of which I have to discuss on Friday night.

I know that the teachers mean well, and that they're doing a phenomenal job with my daughter, but sometimes I wonder whether they realize exactly how many projects they are sending home. I feel like every time I open Adina's knapsack, more projects roll out. I've tried sending her to school without a knapsack, but then the projects come home pinned to her shirt.

Also, almost every week, Adina comes home wearing a hat, which she refuses to take off until it's time to make another hat. Her teachers are experts at coming up with reasons for the children to make hats. But I should point out that these hats don't even perform the regular hat function, which is to keep her head warm. And if I wore a hat like that to shul, they would not let me *daven* for the *amud*.

Also, the Rivkies are very big on having the kids do whatever they want to their projects, so her projects sometimes come home looking like a cat got to them. This is because one of the things we don't let her use at home is safety scissors, so when she gets to school she never puts them down. I've seen projects that looked like they were supposed to be big, beautiful wall signs, but by the time they got home, they were more like wallet size.

Not only that, but some of the projects are pretty much *intended* to be messy – the macaroni projects, anything with glitter, the project they make for *Parshas Lech Lecha* about the stars and the sand – it's like the teachers find it funny to have the children glue whatever random scraps they find lying around the classroom to a piece of paper, using a special kind of non-toxic glue stick that is about as adhesive as wax paper. One time Adina came home with a collage of what I believe was all of the little shreds of paper she'd cut off all of her previous projects. Another time she came home with *milchig* and *fleishig* signs covered in blue and red glitter respectively, and we hung them from our cabinets, and even today we occasionally find ourselves picking glitter out of the *cholent*. And during the fall, Adina learned about squirrels and acorns, and came home with a large paper bag painted to look like a tree, with actual acorns rolling around inside! And to illustrate how the squirrels get the acorns into their paper bags (the squirrels are bag people now), the teachers had helpfully cut big round holes into the sides of the bag! We believe this is how they teach four-year-olds about gravity.

As a result, we have a massive, ever-growing, ever-toppling pile of arts and crafts in our dining room, and I keep trying to thin the pile by throwing out a couple of pieces every night after my daughter goes to bed, except that sometimes she gets up for whatever a four-year-old's reason is to get up, such as to tell me to tuck her in, even though the only reason she's un-tucked is because she got up to tell me to tuck her in, and she'll notice her projects in the garbage and look up at me, all teary-eyed, like, "You didn't like my project?" I never know how to respond to this in a way that a four-year-old can understand, so I fish it out of the garbage and blow off whatever remnants of supper are still attached, and then put it back into the pile, and wait around for another couple of weeks until her baby brother tries to eat it (he usually attacks the macaroni projects first) and ends up chewing it to pieces, at which point we *have* to throw it out. This is why Hashem created baby brothers.

My wife and I have differing ideas as to how to deal with this issue. My wife's idea was to run out and buy a huge plastic box in which to keep all of Adina's projects, the idea being that we would let Adina sort through them at the end of the year and decide which pieces she wanted to keep, and which she found too juvenile. This worries me. What if she decides to keep all of them? Plus, sealing them in a box will make it that much harder for the baby to eat them.

So my idea, which I am thinking of suggesting to my wife, is that we should take whatever projects Adina makes at home or at the crafts store, pin them to her shirt, and send them right back to school. Let the *morahs* find some creative and educational way to deal with them – they can put them up on the walls, they can stick them to the little pretend fridge in the kitchen area, whatever. We could basically send our daughter back and forth, back and forth, all year long, transporting loads of projects, until the teachers surrender and start having the kids make little white flags to bring home. Or else they can start teaching the kids about the wonders of recycling.

Personally, I think it's a great idea. I'm going to start with the huge box.

I remember the first time I ever heard of an open house. I was about ten at the time, and my parents were trying to sell their high ranch. I don't think anyone actually came to look at the house, because it was still on the market for several years afterward, until my grandfather bought it out of mercy. But I do remember that they put out pastries. My mother makes awesome pastries. If my parents ever sell their current house, I urge you to stop by and pretend to be interested, just for the pastries.

But when a local yeshiva recently had *their* open house, they didn't serve *any* pastries. At least I assume they didn't, because my wife didn't bring any home with her. Our daughter is officially supposed to start school soon, and we're having a hard time deciding which school she should attend. Whenever we ask any of the parents about any of these schools, they give us glowing reports about how it is literally the best school in the world, and how happy they are that Hashem blessed them with children just so that they could have the opportunity to be a part of that school. But five minutes later we hear them going on to the other parents about how the school's policies are ridiculous, and how the faculty would not know proper *chinuch* if it went up and bit them on the nose. (Does proper *chinuch* bite people on the nose? I've never seen it.)

Understandably, we're a little indecisive. Luckily, some of the schools run open house events, where prospective parents can come in and see what the school is really like after hours when they've given the students the day off and paid the cleaning staff double overtime and covered up all of the holes in the walls with arts and crafts.

As soon as I found out about the open house, I decided that it was very important to send my wife. I personally did not want to go, because when I go to these things, the thinking portion of my brain shuts down, and I become very eager to please. Back when we were looking at houses, I expressed a sincere interest in buying almost every house that we looked at, because I was afraid of making the current owners feel bad. We looked at one house that had a couple of bedrooms where you could maybe fit one bed each, but only if you kept it folded, and the only way to get into the living room was to jump over the back of the couch, and the guest room was occupied by at least four live birds, and I kept walking around the house and making offers and saying things like, "Wow, what a cute little room!" and "What are those on the wall, shoeprints? It's like a motif!" and "Do the birds come with the guest room? Because I have in-laws." So all in all, I think we were afraid that if I had gone to this thing, I probably would have put down an offer on the school. And that would have been prohibitive, because it was a new building.

In fact, over the course of the evening, the newness of the building was stressed repeatedly. There was even a picture of it in the brochure that my wife brought home –one of those computer-generated models that every school has hanging on the wall when you come in until they actually get to their bigger building with bigger walls, on which they can immediately hang a picture of a much bigger building. These pictures look exactly like what the real school will look like, except that there are evenly-spaced shrubs out in front and there is no long line of honking minivans in the driveway, nor is there a spot on the lawn where the grass is missing because of the time that the third-grade teacher was absent and the class spent the entire day digging what appeared to be a hole to China. These pictures are always taken from some angle that would be impossible in real life without uprooting several major trees and houses and renting a helicopter. So although this particular school already had an actual building of which to take a picture, they chose instead to go with the more perfect computerized model, seeing as they had already been using it on their stationery ever since they moved into their *previous* location, because they couldn't very well have a picture in their logo of the back of a shul.

So even though I did not actually attend the program, I did study all of the paperwork that my wife brought home, and I learned that the school had a lot of the aspects that one might look for in a good school, such as a color copy machine. Back when I was in preschool, we didn't have color copy machines, and look how *I* turned out. We just had black and white copiers, so that when the *morahs* would print out pictures on the weekly *parshah*, we would all have to color them in ourselves. This wasted valuable time that we could have spent learning Gemara, or digging holes.

But these brochures definitely have a lot of pictures. There is one picture of a little girl using a purple crayon, who, upon closer examination, appears to be coloring on her desk. And of course there is the obligatory classroom picture wherein all of the children are pretending to be engrossed in their *chumashim*, but you can just tell that every single one of them is trying his hardest not to acknowledge that there is a photographer in the room, and that the *rebbi* definitely has not stopped teaching because of some photographer, so not one of those children will actually walk out of the classroom knowing that *passuk*.

But mainly, the brochures were dedicated to explaining the yeshivah's views on preschool education. They talked about instilling a love of learning -- I would guess because at some point they looked around at the older grades and found that mainly what the kids had was a love of recess. They also used a lot of big words, such as saying "small manipulatives" when they really meant "Lego". I always thought that *children* were small manipulatives.

There were also a bunch of speeches given at the program, which, according to my wife, primarily stressed the importance of teaching each child on his or her individual level. Every school goes on about the individual levels, which is very ideal in theory, but very hard in practice. None of them ever actually come out and say,

Open House

"Look, we believe in individual levels, but you have to understand that the teacher has to deal with twenty-five other kids, so if your fourth grader keeps acting up, then his individual level will be in the principal's office."

The school also gave out contact forms, which my wife didn't fill out, because we would prefer not to be hassled for money, at least until we can figure out which particular school we would prefer to hassle us. I would like to say that we are closer to making a decision, but we are not, because, as nice as the faculty made it sound, we do realize that they were, by definition, putting their best foot forward. But it was definitely less stressful than coming in during school hours for one of those one-on-one meetings, where the child gets tested on letter recognition and coloring etiquette, and the parents get tested on impromptu math skills. There's no telling what I would blurt out at one of *those*.

Teachers Are Parents, Too

My daughter is starting school this year, and it's my job, as her father, to hunt for school supplies. It's only a little better than uniform shopping. I have been going from store to store for the past few weeks looking for a two-inch, soft-covered loose-leaf binder. I don't even think they *make* those. It must have been added to the list as a practical joke. All the ones I can find that are that big are hard-covered. Why do they need soft covers? Have the kids been injuring themselves on the hard ones?

And on top of all of this, I'm running around looking for my *own* supplies, because I'm a teacher, as it turns out. Really. Ninth, tenth, and eleventh grade Language Arts, at a *mesivta* that shall remain nameless because they don't pay me enough to advertise. I'm the one who marks the essays.

I started teaching in the middle of last year, when I got a call from the English principal (meaning he was the principal of English Studies; he wasn't actually English,) saying, "Do you want to teach?" I wasn't about to say no, because I have a lifelong fear of principals. As I later found out, the students had scared off the previous teacher, Mr. Becker, who clearly had no idea what he was getting into, because the first day of school he came in on a bike. I have no formal training as a teacher, but I assume that one of the first things they teach you in teacher school (which is a funny mental picture in the first place), is that you shouldn't give the students anything to make fun of, because they'll never drop it, ever. If you must use a bike, park it around the corner, or leave it in the trunk of your car. Mr. Becker also gave them other things to make fun of, between his helmet and his name tags and his Shakespeare fixation, and by the time they were done with him, he couldn't bike out of there fast enough.

So I was basically dropped on my head in the middle of the year at about the same time that I started my regular gig as a humor columnist. I was given three classes of thirty students each, which meant that I had to lug around 80,000 pounds of teacher's edition textbooks, and every night I had three lessons to plan, and ninety papers to mark. So I never really got a chance to come up with a grand lesson plan. The plan was more like, "Let's just try to make it through the day and hope that somebody learns *something*."

And it did not help that I had not seen a lot of the material myself since high school. I had to stay at least one step ahead of the kids. I would walk into the classroom and say something like, "Everyone read the textbook, pages 121 to 145, and then STOP READING! I don't want anyone coming in tomorrow, asking me questions from the end of the book!" But there was always one kid who read ahead anyway. "What's an antecedent?" And I would have to sneak glances at my book and try to figure things out quickly. "Um, it's something you take when you have stomach problems. Maybe we'll get to it, if you stop asking so many questions."

But the questions weren't even the problem. What I found out early on, after a few failed attempts to lighten the load once in a while by doing something a little more fun, is that there is really only one thing that high school boys want in an English class, and that is to not be there. This was especially punctuated by one guy, who asked me every single day when I came in whether we were having a free period. Actually, that's not the way he asked it. What he said was, "I heard that we're having a free period today, correct?" Like one day he was going to catch me off-guard, and I'd say, "Yes...um, I mean, no." "Too late." One day I actually said to him, "If I *were* going to give you a free period, do you think I would even bother showing up? Do I really need to stand outside and watch you fight over the basketball court?" The truth was that I didn't really need many days off, because I was already getting all of the days that I wanted anyway, which were Purim, Chol Hamoed, and the summer.

Many of the students could not have made it any more obvious that they did not want to be there. Toward the end of my ninth grade class every day, a number of the guys would sit casually at their desks with one leg stretched way out, pointed at the door, like they were about to sprint off for a marathon. After recess, I would teach the tenth grade, where a good portion of the class would stroll in

Teachers Are Parents, Too

late and cluster around me, and it would smell like the room itself had just played a game of basketball against, say, the lunchroom. And in my eleventh grade class, which was the last period of the day, the guys would sometimes just disappear into thin air. One moment they were sitting there, and the next, they were gone. I wouldn't see them leave, the door would still be closed, and all that would be left of them would be their pens, spinning in midair.

That is, assuming they *had* pens. A lot of the guys showed up to class without any supplies at all, and then, when I handed out an assignment, they got this quizzical look on their faces, like, "You expect me to have a pen and paper? Here in class?" So they'd ask if they could go out to get one, which of course was an excuse to leave, because their lockers were very clearly right there in the classrooms. I've had students hand in papers written in crayon, and one of my students once did his entire assignment in board marker. It soaked straight through the paper to his desk, and I could read it from across the room. Also, some of the students turn in their papers written on the backs of other papers. And one time, one of my students wrote an entire essay in tiny little letters at the top of a piece of paper. So I told him that the bottom half of the paper came free with the top half, and he said that he was saving the bottom for his next essay.

This is not to say that I didn't have any good students. There were a *lot* of good students, some of whom said that they had learned more from me than they did from any other Language Arts teacher they'd ever had, but not in the subject of how to control a class. I feel bad that I couldn't teach them even more, and I plan to try harder this year. For instance, I am thinking of writing up a supplies list. Here it is:

- Writing implement (any)
- Paper (blank)
- Deodorant (or air freshener)
- 64 crayons

In addition, I also hope to have some kind of lesson plan. But I haven't gotten around to starting on it, because I am in the middle of a major scavenger hunt. Does anybody know where I can find a three-pocket folder?

Nobody likes Parent-Teacher Conferences.

The children, of course, don't like it, because most kids get by in school on what experts call "The Nothing System". This means that whatever question their parents ask them about school, the answer is always, "Nothing."

"What did you learn in school today?" "Nothing."

"Did anything interesting happen?" "Nothing."

"The principal left a message earlier. What did he want to speak to me about?" "Nothing."

But the kids know that a Parent-Teacher Conference (PTA, for short) threatens the very fabric of The Nothing System, because when the parents ask the teachers those same questions, the teachers are not going to shrug their shoulders and say, "Nothing." In fact, from the child's experience, the teacher absolutely *loves* to talk, and will tell the parents so much about the child that they will eventually become bored and start passing notes to each other and doodling on the back of the report card. And then the parents will know *everything*.

Meanwhile, the principal, who arranges the whole Conference, doesn't really like it either, because he has to spend the whole time walking around and making small talk with the parents, and he has to pretend, when any parent asks, that he has any idea who their child is out of the 800 kids he has roaming around his halls every day. He only arranges the Conference in the first place because all of the parents expect it.

But the parents don't want to be there either. Sure, there are the younger parents, who are all excited because this is their very first child, and they show up as a couple and smile a lot and bring along big yellow legal pads. But then the teacher tells them that their child is not, in fact, the smartest child on the face of the planet, and eventually they turn into cynical parents who don't want to be there, like everybody else.

But the process has definitely evolved to make things easier for the parents. For the longest time, it worked like this: You would show up and try to find a parking spot in a lot where every space said "Teacher Parking", and you would be made to stand in these long, depression-era style lines, which often did not appear to be moving at all, and so periodically you would feel the need to check with the parent in front of you that this was indeed a line to speak to the teacher, rather than a whole bunch of tired people leaning against a wall. These lines were so long that parents started to have flashbacks to their school days, when they had to wait in line for mundane things such as the right to come in from recess. So there'd be a lot of cutting and shoving and saving of spaces among all the parents, and the principal would have to stop making small talk and come over to settle things, and then he would have to call up some of the grandparents to come to school and pick up the parents.

But best-case scenario, Parent-Teacher Conferences consisted of a bunch of lines of bored, scowling parents, clutching report cards or staring at them for the fourth time in five minutes, as if they would suddenly be able to make out what the teacher wrote in the "comments" section.

"What does that say? Is that even a word? 'Chaim needs to work on his *something*.' That's helpful."

So what the schools started doing, at some point, was coordinate the meetings alphabetically, so that if your last name was Aardvark, you would come in at eight o'clock, and if your last name was Zwyzowsky, you would come in at eleven-thirty the following Tuesday. But this was a problem for those parents—and there are many of them in the Jewish community—who had more than one child, meaning that all of their meetings were scheduled for exactly the same time. And invariably, one child's teacher would decide that people like the Zwyzowskys were always getting a raw deal, and decide to do the whole thing reverse alphabetically, so that, besides for the M's and the N's, all of the parents would have to go home and come back, sometimes several times if any of the other teachers decided to go by the *alef-beis*. So generally, what most parents do these days is they come for the first scheduled meeting, and then they form lines for all of the others. So things haven't really changed, except that the M's and the N's have no shot at parking spaces.

Of course, some of your veteran parents have strategies to help minimize the wait. For instance, some of them show up together, like all of your younger couples, but instead of sitting in on all of the meetings together ("You're wrong! Our *sheifeleh is* the smartest child on the face of the planet!"), they bring along walkie-talkies, and possibly a beach chair, so that one parent can wait in all of the lines while the other parent swoops in at the last minute and meets with the teachers. In fact, sometimes it helps to show up with a whole *busload* of relatives.

Meanwhile, the teachers don't have it any better. I myself am a teacher, which totally trumps the fact that I am technically also a young parent, because I go through enough meetings in one night to make me just as bitter as everyone else. I teach high school boys how to write, but not how to write like me, because I don't need the competition as soon as everyone graduates.

But the truth is that I have no idea what to say to most of the parents, aside from repeating the same little speech about how I propose to teach writing skills to a bunch of teenagers who give one-word answers to every question. (WRITE AN ESSAY ABOUT WHAT YOU DID ON YOUR SUMMER VACATION: "Nothing.") I figure that I have to say at least one good thing and one not-so-good thing about every child, because if I say only good things, the parents will give me the same skeptical look that they give the principal when he tells them, "Your son must be good, because I don't know who he is."

But how do I say the not-so-good things to the parents' faces, especially when I don't want them to get upset and call for backup? And so I (and many other teachers) come up with a bunch of code phrases that on the surface sound like compliments, so that it's not until the parents get home that they realize that I actually said something controversial about their son. Here are some examples, with the subtitles put in:

- "He's extremely thorough."

  I have to stay late every day so he can hand in his assignment.

- "He's very enthusiastic."

  Seriously. I can't get him to stop talking.

- "He has a great singing voice."

  I shouldn't know this. I'm his writing teacher.

- "He's very spirited."

  How do I get him to stop cheering?

- "He doesn't make any noise."

  Is he even listening? I have no idea. He won't tell me.

- "He always hands in the work of everyone in his row."

  I'm pretty sure he's copying from someone.

So no one really likes Parent-Teacher Conferences. Yet we continue to have them, despite the fact that we are living in an age of phones. And also, call waiting, which is just like waiting in line, but with elevator music.

Not Rocket Science

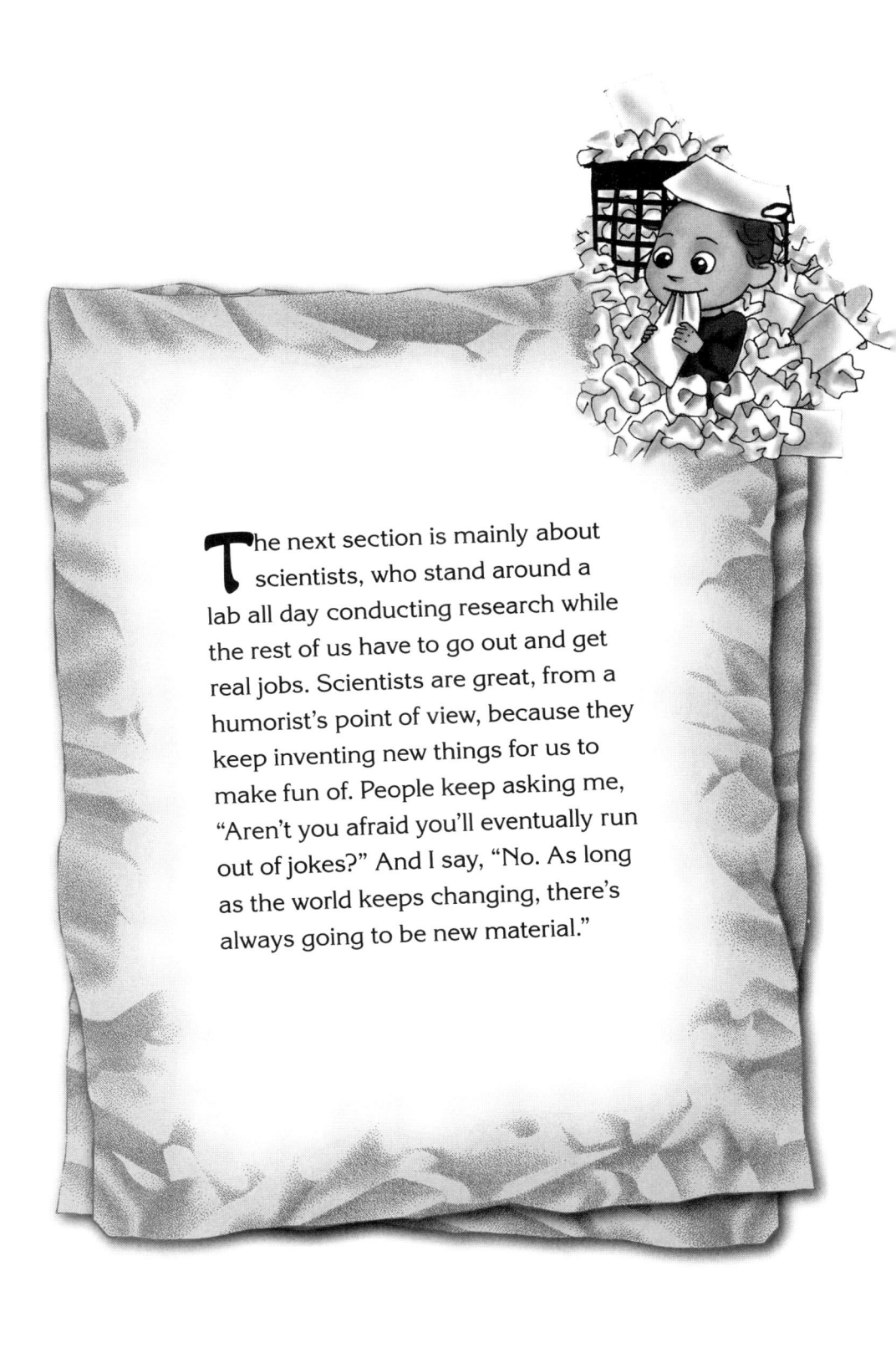

The next section is mainly about scientists, who stand around a lab all day conducting research while the rest of us have to go out and get real jobs. Scientists are great, from a humorist's point of view, because they keep inventing new things for us to make fun of. People keep asking me, "Aren't you afraid you'll eventually run out of jokes?" And I say, "No. As long as the world keeps changing, there's always going to be new material."

I think that technology might be dumbing us down. Take Satellite Navigational Systems, for example. A Satellite Navigational System, or "GPS" for short, is a device that hooks up to your dashboard and uses satellites up in space to tell you where you are, as opposed to just letting you ask your wife here on Earth. The device also has a feature wherein if you enter a destination address, a friendly voice will tell you exactly where to go, where to turn, etc., to the point where you want to actually obey the traffic laws, because you realize that what you are doing is visible from space. (There is a *mussar vort* here somewhere.)

Although this device is very convenient, a lot of the people who use it seem to lose some very essential life skills. My uncle has a

GPS, because he is a life insurance salesman, and if you want to make it as a life insurance salesman, you have to honestly believe that your client may not last long enough for you to drive all the way over to his house if you have to look up directions first. But we ran into problems when I called to tell him about my son's *bris* a few years back.

"What's the address?" he wanted to know.

"I don't know," I said. "It's on the corner. It's a big white building."

"That doesn't help me," he said, "Do you think I can just type in, 'Big White Building on the Corner'?"

"No," I said. "How about you just look for the big white building on the corner?"

The truth is, I *like* giving directions. I *like* saying things like, "Make a left at the gas station," and, "If you have to pay a toll, then you've gone too far." But technology's getting rid of that. Technology is getting rid of the skill of finding things on your own, and the skill of stopping people on the street to ask for directions, and the skill of helping your wife understand that you're not actually lost, and the skill of making up time by driving faster, and the skill of explaining things to the cops.

There was a story in the paper recently about a man in Germany who, at the advice of his GPS, made a left turn onto a set of railroad tracks, and his wheels got stuck. Twelve trams were delayed because of him, and delaying trams is a federal offense in Germany.

Now I'm not saying that it was his fault. I have no doubt that this particular GPS was speaking in German, and when you hear a voice yelling, "*Mach a linx! A linx!*" you make a *linx* and worry about the consequences later. But there are also *other* stories of people who blindly followed their GPS without bothering to check things for themselves. There was a story of another man in Germany whose GPS steered him right into a construction zone, and he crashed into a pile of sand. There was also a man in Britain who was driving at night, and his GPS told him there was a bridge ahead, but what the device didn't realize was that it was not actually a bridge, but a ferry for cars, and that the ferry was not actually at the dock at the moment, and so the man drove straight off the loading dock into the canal. Like it or not, these devices *do* make mistakes.

My friend's uncle was once driving toward a new bridge, and his GPS was convinced that there was no bridge there. "Warning," it said. "Water ahead." But he just kept driving. So the device tried again, a little louder. "WARNING!" But this guy knew there was a bridge, so he just kept driving. Eventually, the device was screaming at full blast: "WATER AHEAD! WATER AHEAD! ABORT! ABORT!" If it were able to, the device probably would have leaped out the passenger door and hit the ground rolling. But finally, the driver got over the bridge, and the GPS stopped and regained its composure. "Make your next right," it said, as if nothing had happened.

Sure, don't apologize or anything.

But GPS systems are not the only inventions that have been dumbing us down. Thanks to calculators, over seventy-five percent of the population – that's nearly one half – can no longer do math in their heads. Calculators were originally invented to help us with complex problems, and to write words upside down using only numbers. But people don't know when to stop. People don't know how to spell these days either, thanks to spell-check, and this is despite proven evidence that spell-check doesn't exactly know what it's talking about. For instance, as I write this article, my spell-check is insisting, using a squiggly red line, that there is no such word as "dumbing". But I'm ignoring it, because it also tells me that there's no such thing as a "Mordechai."

Also, thanks to technology, we don't actually have to remember anything. Our phones hold phone numbers, our palms hold addresses, and there are services wherein you tell them your wife's birthday or your anniversary, and every year on that date they will send over flowers and a card, so that you can come home from work with absolutely no clue why your wife is suddenly in a good mood, and are afraid to ask, because you're just thankful that she's not blasting you again for leaving your socks on the floor in two different rooms.

Also, some technologies are making us rude, besides for the GPS devices that won't apologize when they basically come out and yell, "*We're all gonna die!*" while you're trying to carry on an important business call on your cell phone. In fact, thanks to cell phones, it is now socially acceptable to talk to oneself on the street. Also, sometimes you find yourself with an actual living person who has chosen instead to talk to someone that you have no idea exists, because you can't see the earpiece, and you think they are actually talking to you, but they are so engrossed in their conversation that they don't notice that you are answering every single question they are asking the other party, until they ask a question that makes no sense, and you call them on it, and they suddenly go, "What? Oh, sorry, I'm on the phone." When this happens, I am tempted to call them from *my* cell phone, so that they can put the other person on hold and finish our conversation. But that would just be rude.

Losing RAM

Of course, some will argue that technology is not actually making us dumber; it is just giving us new skills at the expense of our old ones. For instance, we can no longer remember phone numbers, but we know how to operate a cell phone. And we can no longer focus on any one specific thing, but we have learned to multi-task. In fact, scientists at the Institute of Research and More Research have recently conducted a study on the ability of people nowadays to focus on any one thing. By the end of the first week, they reported that people are fifty percent less likely to stay focused than they used to be, and by the end of the second week we have no idea what happened, because the scientists had stopped monitoring.

Is my point that technology is bad? Of course not. We *love* technology. It's the best thing since sliced bread. In fact, technology is what sliced the bread in the first place. Rather, my point is... Well, I seem to have forgotten my point. I blame technology.

It's tough to be a scientist. Sometimes you can labor away on a project for years, coming up with innovation after innovation, losing yourself in your work, and when you're finally done, you look around and realize that nobody cares. The Nobel Prize Committee takes one look at your project, and decides that, as ingenious as it was, your "Analysis of People's Brainwave Patterns While Chewing Different Flavors of Gum" is not really going to make the world a better place. But does that mean that your work is any less important than, say, the invention of penicillin?

Yes. Of course it does. But that did not stop the people at *The Annals of Improbable Research* (*AIR*) from coming up with an

How Ignoble of You

annual awards ceremony dedicated to honoring these discoveries. *AIR* is a group that publishes a newsletter featuring the scientific equivalence of Purim Torah. For instance, they once conducted a study comparing apples to oranges with the aid of an electron microscope, and they discovered that the two were not quite as dissimilar as many would have them believe. They also pointed out that if you make a comparison that has absolutely nothing to do with apples and oranges, and someone tells you that you are comparing apples to oranges, then that person is, in fact, comparing apples to oranges.

In 1991, *AIR* developed the Ig Nobel Prizes, based on the word "ignoble", meaning "horrible", and Alfred Nobel, who established the Nobel Peace Prize after inventing dynamite. *AIR* developed the prize to prove the scientific idiom that some people have *way* too much spare time on their hands.

But the Ig Nobels are awarded only for real achievements. For instance, one year David Schmidt of the University of Massachusetts won the Physics prize for his analysis of why shower curtains tend to billow inwards -- especially the rarely-cleaned ones that are turning brown at the bottom -- so that you find yourself basically hugging the far wall of the shower as the curtain keeps advancing on you. (Most people think about their day in the shower, but David thinks about showers in the shower.) He basically came to the conclusion that it has to do with high and low pressure systems, and wrote up a report that included a weather map of his shower.

The Ig Nobels garnered media attention in 2004, when a bunch of students at the University of Illinois won the prize for Public Health by investigating the scientific validity of the Five-Second Rule. The Five-Second Rule states that any food that is picked up within five seconds of being dropped on the floor will have collected such a small amount of bacteria that it could easily be killed by the acids in your stomach. This is what's known as a "polite fiction". Another one is, "No! I was just scratching my upper lip," or "No! I'm offering *everyone* breath mints."

In general, the Five-Second Rule is only applied by the person who actually drops the food, and even then, it depends on how good the food tastes. Cookies, for instance, have the Five-Second Rule, while mashed potatoes don't. The rule also depends on how long it takes you to pick up your food. My one-year-old son, for example, has a Six-Day Rule. And then there are the people who believe that you can get the bacteria off the bottom of a cookie by blowing on it.

As part of their experiment, the students went around the university swabbing at random floors with Q-tips, and then analyzed them under a microscope, and what they found amazed them: the floors had exactly the same bacteria as the apples and oranges.

Just kidding. In actuality, they found that most dry floors are actually okay. But then they smeared a floor with E. Coli, and the results were pretty scary. So the moral of the story is that you should not eat at any of their houses, or use their Q-tips.

Over the years, the Ig Nobel Prize Committee has recognized some pretty hefty achievements. Among them:

- In 1996, Robert Matthews of England won the prize for Physics for his studies of why toast always lands buttered-side down. According to Matthews, this happens because our tables are generally not high enough for the toast to

How Ignoble of You

complete an entire rotation before landing. He theorizes that if we were to eat off of tables that were six feet high, our toast would have an even chance of landing right side up, although to be fair, we would also be dropping it more. Of course, none of this matters if you hold of the Five-Second Rule.

If we want to solve the toast problem, Matthews says, we can try making our toast smaller – say, the size of a quarter, smearing our butter on the underside of the bread, or tying it to the back of a cat. Otherwise, he says, if we notice a piece of toast sliding off our plates, we could stop it from flipping over by quickly swatting it down to the floor, although not in public, and definitely not at the University of Illinois.

- In 1999, Hyuk-Ho Kwon of South Korea won the prize for Environmental Protection for inventing a self-perfuming business suit, thus allowing people to dash off to work in the mornings without having to wrestle with the shower curtain. The suits retain their aroma through about forty dry-cleanings, and can be made to smell like pine, lavender, peppermint, and a new car.

- In 1998, Troy Hubris of Ontario won the award for Safety Engineering, by developing and personally testing a suit of armor designed to be impervious to grizzly bears. Apparently this is a problem up in Canada. The suit, which weighs about 175 pounds, is made from rubber, chain mail, and steel, and makes the wearer look like he went a little overboard with the latkes. Troy spent years building and testing the suit, letting bikers beat him up, throwing himself off cliffs, etc., and when he finally got to test it with a real live bear, the bear freaked out and spent the entire time cowering at the other end of the cage. Maybe he should have made it smell like maple syrup or something.

- In 2003, the Physics Prize was awarded to a long list of people in Australia for writing a report entitled, "An Analysis of the Forces Required to Drag Sheep Over Various Surfaces."

Okay. We bet these guys are really fun at parties. ("Alright, everyone! Let's all drag our sheep over to the buffet table.")

More recently, we are pleased to announce, the laureates were just as interesting, and since then, they've showed no signs of letting up. Two professors at the University of California won an award for explaining why woodpeckers don't get headaches. This research could be valuable to anyone who is reading this article and wants to bang his head against the wall, but is afraid of getting a headache. Meanwhile, three professors at Northwestern University received a medal for conducting experiments to learn why people dislike the sound of fingernails scraping across a blackboard. It's awesome when a teacher can do that to his entire class in the name of science. And finally, the Mathematics Prize was awarded to Nic Svenson and Piers Barnes of Australia (there must be something in the water over there) for calculating how many photographs a person has to take to ensure that no one in the group will have their eyes closed. After much banging their heads against the wall, the answer they came up with was: One billion. And even more if someone in the group is wearing a perfumed business suit.

A Sense of Academia

In general, way too many of us take our five senses for granted. If you are ever walking down the street and you see someone smiling, chances are he's taking his senses for granted. If I were you, I would walk right up and give him a *potch*. Fortunately, though, there are people out there who are, at this very moment, conducting research to better help us understand and appreciate our senses and to help out people who are not as fortunate.

Take for example, the AP article dated December 27th entitled, "Scientists Study Human Olfactory Ability". For the benefit of those of you who basically open up the newspaper and head straight for the comics, the article discusses a group of psychology students at Berkeley College in California who, at the behest of their professors, got down on their hands and knees on the college lawn and sniffed out a thirty-foot-long trail of chocolate scent. The article does not say how the professors got the students to do this, but these are psychology professors we are dealing with, so they figured something out. We're guessing that it was a really nice day, and they gave the class a choice between crawling around on the lawn, and sitting in a stuffy classroom discussing how everyone felt about not being able to go outside.

The way the study worked was, the scientists soaked some ropes in chocolate essence, which is the same stuff that they spray on the ground in front of candy stores to get you to walk in even though you very clearly don't want to, and they laid the ropes in random patterns on the ground. Then, to make sure that the students would use only their sense of smell to follow the rope, the professors provided blindfolds, gloves, kneepads, elbow pads, and earmuffs (so they wouldn't hear the ropes, I guess). The professors then sat back on lawn chairs and relished in the fact that they did not have to prepare a lesson, and watched their charges sniff around in a zigzag pattern and occasionally bump into each other. In the meantime, each student was chugging along at an average of two-to-three-hundred sniffs per minute and picking up all sorts of pollen and dust and small, harmless insects, and secretly wondering if he was part of some elaborate college prank wherein all of the other students had secretly walked off or were filming him with their cell phones.

The zigzag pattern, says Professor Noam Sobel of Berkeley, was caused by the students comparing the scents coming in from both nostrils to figure out where the smell was coming from, the same way we compare the noise levels coming in from both of our ears to find out where a sound is originating. If our nostrils were situated front-to-back, there would be no zigzag pattern, but we would probably brush our teeth more often.

Sobel says that most researchers have felt that people cannot compare scents because our nostrils are too close together. Never mind the fact that some people's ears are too close together, and it doesn't stop them. Of the thirty-two students who participated in the experiment, two-thirds made it all of the way to the end of the rope, and the other third ended up in the cafeteria.

As the next part of the experiment, the students had to repeat this procedure with one of their nostrils taped shut. This time, only one-third of the students got to the end of their rope, while the rest presumably ended up sniffing in little frantic circles. But from a psychological standpoint, the experiment was a total success. As a final measure, Sobel had the students wear small electronic filtering devices on their noses, but by that point everyone was at the end of their rope. At least we assume this was the case, because there were only four students left for that last assignment, but that could be because Sobel had only four devices to go around, and no one wanted to take turns.

Sobel said that he hopes to use his findings to develop eNose – a robot that tracks smells. We could think of plenty of uses for this robot, such as when we get back to our house after a vacation and open the front door and are almost knocked backwards down the steps by an unidentified odor that was definitely not there when we left. But with eNose, we could simply send the robot into the house to find the source of the smell and get rid of it. Of course, then we'd have to schlep eNose along on our vacations, and they'd probably kick us out of most of the motels we went to. Also, we live in New Jersey, so the moment we switched it on, it would probably have a nervous breakdown.

Another point of his experiments, says Sobel, is to see if humans can further develop their sense of smell. We're sure that the parents of these students are thrilled that they're shelling out thousands of dollars per year so that when their children graduate, they can come back home and put their talents to work by sniffing out leftovers in the fridge. Although it would definitely make *bedikas chametz* easier.

Our other story involves a January 1st AP article concerning a handful of universities in New Jersey and Pennsylvania that have taken in a bunch of seven-week-old dogs. But before you start thinking about how schools seem to be relaxing their admission standards a bit more every year, we should probably explain that these dogs are being trained by the students of these colleges for a future as seeing-eye dogs for the blind.

According to a guide-dog training school called The Seeing Eye, which is based out of Morristown, the idea is to get the dogs acclimated to being around as many noisy people in as short a time as possible, as well as to teach them to sit perfectly still and doze off in forty-five minute increments. The students, meanwhile, are more than happy with the prospect of having dogs in their classes, because some of the teachers like to grade on a curve. Plus, there's always the possibility that one of the dogs will eat their homework.

The article goes on to state that The Seeing Eye has a similar program worked out with prisons. Prisons? Is that really the best idea? What if the idea backfires, and the dogs learn to defend themselves? And how long does it take to train a dog to stop chasing the license-plate machine?

So our idea, rather than to send innocent puppies to prison, is to combine the two universities' programs. We picture an ear-muffed, blindfolded student crawling around in the grass and sniffing, all the while being led on a leash by a dog, who is also sniffing. At the moment, we are still unsure whether it would be better, or at least more fun, not to tell the students about this development beforehand, and to let them figure it out on their own. (*Sniff, sniff.* "Do you smell dogs?") It would then be the student's responsibility to teach his dog not to eat the rope. And it would be the professors' job to keep track of how many of the students are still on school grounds by the time the experiment is over.

So maybe we should quit while we're ahead.

Chicken Soup For The Stomach

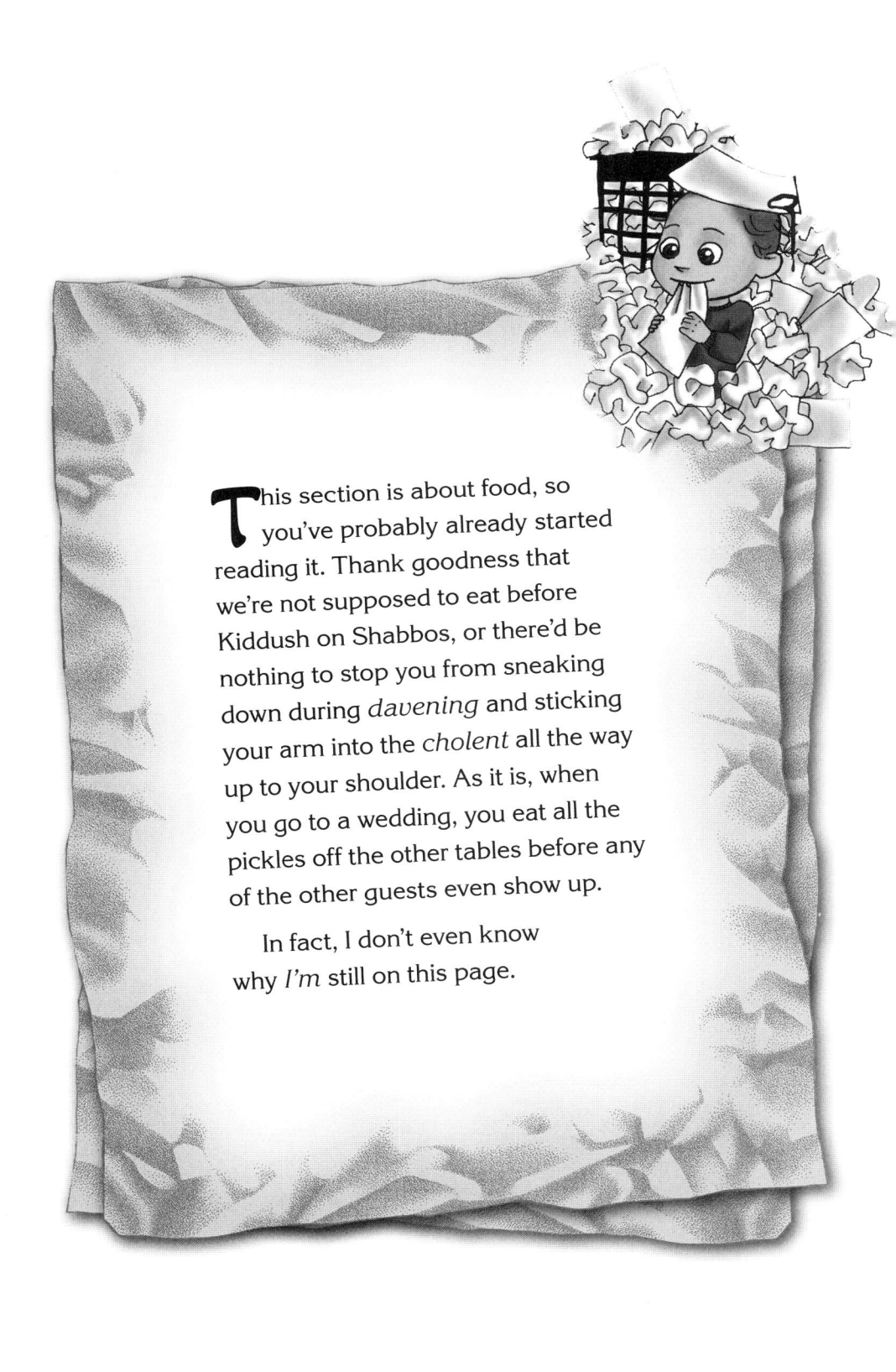

This section is about food, so you've probably already started reading it. Thank goodness that we're not supposed to eat before Kiddush on Shabbos, or there'd be nothing to stop you from sneaking down during *davening* and sticking your arm into the *cholent* all the way up to your shoulder. As it is, when you go to a wedding, you eat all the pickles off the other tables before any of the other guests even show up.

In fact, I don't even know why *I'm* still on this page.

I think it's about time I wrote an article about trans fats.

For most of my life, I've put about as much thought into my weight as trailer park residents put into hurricanes. Sure, they're aware that hurricanes exist, at least on some level, and they're also aware, because they asked around, that the previous occupants of that exact spot had their house blown away while they were out buying "hurricane supplies", which should have included a ship anchor. But they figure, "That's not going to happen to us."

Growing up, I was the same way, only much thinner. I had such a high metabolism that eating junk food actually made me lose weight. I have no idea where all of the food was going, but it had to go somewhere. I think it was going into other people. I was one of those kids who always ended up on top of the seesaw, begging the other kid to please let me down gently. I have a lot of childhood memories of shrieking and slamming into the ground.

But over the past few years, it seems that I may have been steadily putting on a few pounds. At least that's what my wife is saying. But I think that deep down, every woman believes that her husband could stand to lose a few pounds, even if he's so thin that he occasionally falls through sidewalk grates.

I, personally, am in denial about my weight, and plan to be in denial for the foreseeable future. I still avoid low-fat mayonnaise and skim milk, I still believe in teaching my children about the wonders of Shabbos Party, and I still buy pants in the same size that I did when I got married, only now I buy the kind with the stretchy waistbands. I do occasionally weigh myself, but I have no idea what the numbers mean, because I don't remember how much I weighed the last time, nor how long it has been since then. Nevertheless, I do remember my wife saying at some point that people's metabolisms change when they have kids, so that could be it. I think this is because all of the food that our children eat goes straight into our bodies.

So these days, because marriage is all about compromise, I try eating less when my wife is around, but that's hard when your job requires you to sit in front of a computer and wait for professional sentences to appear in your brain. I actually find that I write better when I'm chewing on something. I've tried gum, but I tend to get nauseous when it loses its flavor, so the average piece of gum lasts just under two minutes. When I was a kid, I was able to chew on a piece of gum for hours, sometimes days, until I could no longer remember what kind of gum it was or where I got it. That would be a nice amount of gum tolerance to have right about now.

So when I heard that New York was banning trans fats in all of their restaurants, my first thought was, "What's a trans fat?" I imagine many of you had the same question. So I looked up "trans fat" in the encyclopedia, and it said the following:

"Trans fat is monounsaturated or polyunsaturated fat that has been altered by partial hydrogenation."

So there you are.

In English, trans fats are created by forcing hydrogen into a vat of liquid vegetable oil. This is tough, because hydrogen floats, so it keeps trying to get out of the vat, plus it's extremely flammable. That's why, by the time they're done, it's still only *partially* hydrogenated. This process was developed in the early 1900s, and was first commercialized in 1911 as Crisco.

Crisco is weird. I tried it plain once while making a cake – I don't know what I thought it would taste like, but there was a picture of a pie on the front of the container. Turns out, it didn't taste anything like whipped cream, and I had a hard time washing it off my finger. In fact, I still have that very same container, which I have just dug out of the back of the baking closet, and it now has a greenish hue and smells positively awful. I also noticed that most of the prose on the side of the can seems devoted to explaining the benefits of Crisco over butter and margarine, and there are also detailed instructions on what to do if your Crisco catches fire.

The encyclopedia article goes on to talk about how trans fats are also naturally found in the meat and dairy products of animals that ruminate. I'd always thought that the word "ruminate" meant "to think", but it turns out that it also means "to chew one's cud". I guess that's because when you see a cow at the zoo chewing on nothing and staring off into the distance, it looks like it's lost in thought, and you almost feel bad interrupting it to let your two-year-old run his sticky fingers along its back.

(I, too, enjoy ruminating while I ruminate, but I don't want to ruminate on gum.)

But natural trans fats are not the problem. They can even be healthy in moderation. It's the artificial stuff that's the issue, because, aside from the fact that it has a ridiculously long shelf life so long as you don't put your finger bacteria into it and seal the container for four years, trans fats are neither required nor beneficial to one's health.

These days, we Americans are obsessed with dieting. This is because every five minutes, scientists come out with a study that says that with the exception of a select few, we are all hideously overweight. I think that this discovery came about while they were researching fuel efficiency, and they noticed that a staggering amount of Americans drive Sport Utility Vehicles, despite the fact that not many of them actually work in the jungle. So they did some research, and they discovered that the reason so many people drive SUVs is that when they drove around in little cars, the undersides kept scraping along the ground. This was not good, because all of the sparks that this generated could potentially ignite the hydrogen in all of the trans fats that everyone was consuming, and we can't very well have overweight people exploding all over the place. So that was when the government decided to step in.

According to federal law, most companies are now required to put trans fat information on the sides of their containers, right next to the instructions on what to do if the product you are holding catches fire. In mid-2006, New York City tried to get in on this by telling restaurants to voluntarily get rid of trans fats, but when no one volunteered, they made it mandatory. I hate it when parents do that.

So that is where we stand. Personally, I think it's a great idea, in part because I live in New Jersey, but also in part because if you live in New York, and Manhattan especially, you have to be as tall and skinny as possible, like the buildings. People need to be fit so they can run five blocks for the subway and elbow their way past everyone else and squeeze into that one railcar like there's not another train directly behind it. Personally, the best way for *me* to stop gaining weight is to finish writing this article, so I can stop noshing on this Crisco.

Does anyone know how to wash this stuff off a keyboard?

It seems that Coca Cola has released a new type of soda that is actually fortified with vitamins and minerals! "Fat, but healthy" – that's their motto.

Personally, I think it's a great idea, because nowadays it seems that just about everyone is into taking vitamins. Most of us know someone who cannot start their day without first choking down a mountain of pills, such as Iron and Zinc and enough "letter" vitamins to spell out their last names. Some of these, such as the Vitamin-C pills, are about the size of grapefruits, which begs the question of why these people can't just get their vitamin C from an actual grapefruit.

The reason, of course, is that the commonly held belief is that pills are weightless, so people can ingest ten pounds of pills every day, and not have to worry about gaining weight. People are very nervous about their weight these days, because we are in the middle of what health officials are calling the "Obesity *Epidemic*", like it's an outbreak of SARS, and you can catch it from your Bubby's cooking. Like years from now we'll be telling our grandchildren about how we lived through the Obesity Epidemic: "It was horrible. There were carbs and trans fats everywhere. And then there was this thing called "trifle" that could put a moose into a coma. Luckily I survived, thanks to BaHaB."

But it's not Coke's fault that we're fat. In fact, Coke was originally developed, back in the 1880s, to be used as a medicine, probably to cure emaciation. No, we're just kidding. It was actually developed to cure morphine addiction, neurasthenia, headaches (presumably caffeine headaches), and something called dyspepsia, which is a disorder of the stomach – hence the bubbles. (Personally, I think it's funny that Coke was developed to cure dyspepsia.) The man who originally invented it, John Pemberton, distributed it out of his pharmacy in small medicine cups, like schnapps at a kiddush.

But somehow, somewhere along the line, we have gotten to the point where people are drinking soda three meals a day, out of cups large enough to soak their feet in. This is despite the fact that no one really has any idea what's in cola in the first place... Cocoa? Coca leaves? Cola beans? Pepsin? What exactly *are* cola beans, and how come we never see them in a *cholent*? This is as opposed to orange soda, which everyone knows is made from some kind of mutant neon oranges. Also, no doubt everyone has heard of the experiment wherein you put a penny into a bottle of Coke, and within a few days it dissolves, and then the person telling you about the experiment says, "Imagine what it does to your teeth!" (Never mind the fact that:

- Dripping water can do the same thing to a rock,

- In actuality, you need a very high concentration of Coke syrup to dissolve a penny. If you drop a penny into a regular bottle of Coke, what will actually happen is the penny will come out cleaner, with all of the rust and muck cleaned off of it. *Now* imagine what it does to your teeth. And,

- Orange juice does the same thing.)

But none of this is Coke's fault. They're just trying to make a buck. It's not their fault that people can't control themselves. But the truth is that people actually *cannot* help themselves, as is evidenced by the existence of Fried Coke.

Fried Coke was developed for the Texas State Fair by a vendor named Abel Gonzalez Jr., and actually makes us happy that we don't generally go to state fairs. Abel flavored a donut batter with Coke (as opposed to milk or water), deep-fried it, drizzled Coke fountain syrup on it, and topped it all off with whipped cream and cinnamon-sugar, as well as a cherry, for the health nuts. In short, Abel has come up with a product that can make you gain weight just thinking about it, and over the course of a month, he sold over 35,000 of them. (That is why everything is bigger over in Texas.) He tried developing a Fried Pepsi, but he decided it was too sweet. Next year, though, he may try frying Diet Coke, for the people who are watching their weight to an extent.

Obviously, the ones he sells are not kosher, but there is no reason why you can't just whip up a batch of your own for a special occasion, such as when you're having company that you don't want to have again for a while. All you need is about 35,000 liters of Coke and enough whipped cream to fill a swimming pool. I personally would never make it, because I feel guilty enough about drinking soda in the first place. The only things I would ever consider deep-frying are foods that at least start out healthy, such as fish, or eggplant, or potatoes.

Nevertheless, Gonzalez's creation won the prize for creativity at the second annual Big Tex (no kidding) Choice Awards Contest, beating out deep-fried avocadoes, candy apple turnovers, and his last year's entry – the fried peanut butter, jelly, and banana sandwich. Apparently, some people will deep fry just about anything that isn't moving. Target actually sells a deep fryer that can take a whole turkey, or, I would guess, a watermelon.

So the prevailing theory is that Coke rushed into this vitamins and minerals thing in order to counteract any negative publicity they might have gotten for the Fried Coke incident from the Organization of People Who Will Eat Anything at State Fairs, Even Things They'd Never Heard Of, And Then Maybe Think About It Later. Their new product, called "Diet Coke Plus", contains niacin, vitamins B6 and B12, magnesium, and zinc. Pepsi came out with a similar soda later in the year called "Tava", which sounds dangerously like "*taivah*", and which contains Vitamins B3, B6, E, and chromium.

Chromium? Don't just throw metal in for metal's sake. Sounds like we're taking this "minerals" thing too literally.

In short, Coke and Pepsi are advertising their sodas as totally healthy, and part of a complete breakfast, except for the fact that NutraSweet can kill you. Also, it still totally explodes on contact with Mentos. (Don't try that at home. Maybe in someone *else's* home.) Both companies are insistent that the new products not be called "soft drinks", which denotes unhealthiness, but rather "sparkling beverages", which is a politically correct term, like "persons of weight", and "weapons of mass destruction".

So there you have it. Coke has started dropping large quantities of those chewable children's vitamins into vats of Diet Coke to see if will have the same reaction as Mentos, but instead, it's dissolving, like the pennies fail to do. On the bright side, though, it does get rid of that Diet Coke aftertaste – "Mmm, fizzers!"

How Do You Like Them Apples?

If you have kids, you have to go apple picking at least once a year. At least *I* have to. Not that I don't want to. Picking apples is a lot of fun, and you get to teach your children many valuable life lessons, such as that apples are not actually grown at the supermarket, and that you can charge more for produce if you let people pick it themselves. Also, while you're roaming fruitfully around the apple orchard, you get to *fress* out on "All You Can Eat", provided that all you want to eat is apples and you don't really care about washing them.

We visit the apple orchard every year on the Sunday before Rosh Hashanah with our friends, the Weiners, who live in Manhattan and consequently find it very important to come out to New Jersey once a year and teach their kids about trees. Of course, they get offended if I put it that way. "Our kids see trees all the time," they tell us. "What about Central Park?" And once in a while my wife and I come into the city and teach our kids about buildings.

But my problem is that it looks like we're pretty much going to go to this same apple orchard with them every year now. Every family has some place that they go to every so often to meet up with some other family, do the same exact thing, and go home. You did it that first year, and you had a great time, and then you decided to try to recreate that same fun the next year. Only it turned out that the whole fun of the first year was the spontaneity, and so the second year isn't quite as great, even though you retrace every step and have all the same conversations. But no one wants to say anything, so you keep doing it every single year until you start dreading it, but you don't want to say anything because you don't want to offend the other family, who is also not saying anything because they don't want to offend *you*. When I was growing up, my family had at least eight such places, and I went along to every single one of them on every Chol Hamoed and Chanukah until *baruch* Hashem I got married. So now I have my own places that I'm going to go to every year. But luckily, even if we get bored, the place that *we* go to also has an actual purpose, which is to pick apples for Rosh Hashanah. Unfortunately, we really need only about four apples total for Rosh Hashanah, so it really *is* all about the location.

And boy, do we pick apples. That's the other thing about apple picking; there really is not much to do out in the orchard besides pick apples, so by the time you're done, you come home with basically your entire weight in apples. You lug these apples around the orchard in a stroller, which is being constantly chased by your confused toddler, because he assumed that the stroller was for *him*.

Luckily, we had plenty of apples to keep him happy. We had plenty of apples for *everything*, as a matter of fact. That's the other thing about apple picking. When you're at the fruit stand at the beginning of the day, and they ask you how many bags you want to buy, you say to your spouse, "How about one bag per person? Is that enough? Should we get more?" But then you come home with about eight hundred apples and you realize that you have about two weeks before they go bad. So all of a sudden you're eating apples for breakfast, lunch, and supper, you're putting them in pies, and kugels, and soups, and you're handing them out at the door. "Quick, everyone; eat the apples! They're going bad!"

And we have a lot of different kinds of apples, too, not that I can taste the difference. According to the guy who gave us a hayride to the orchard, they grow over twenty different kinds of apples over there, most of which seem, to the untrained eye, to be the same type of apple, except that they grow in different parts of the orchard. I suspect that sometimes, in the middle of the night, the orchard workers dig up all of the trees and switch them around, just to see if anyone can tell the difference. But no one can. The guy on the hayride still thinks that they have certain kinds of apples *this* way, and certain kinds *that* way. Nevertheless, the apple industry wants us to believe that there are many different varieties of apples, because if there aren't, we have no need to buy more than one kind. Just look around the produce department of your supermarket, and you will see such varieties as Red Delicious, Golden Delicious,

Red Okay, Brown Delicious, Rome, Liberty, Empire, Rubashkin, Jonagold, Granny Smith, Bubby Weinstein, Tante Bessie, Seedless, and Clearance. And comparing Granny Smiths to, say, Empires, is like comparing apples to oranges. Okay, it's not *exactly* like comparing apples to oranges. But in the meantime, there are only like two types of grapefruit. So clearly this is all a big scam.

The other thing that we do at the orchard, aside from picking our weight in apples and trying to sample twenty apples just to see if we can taste the difference, is hold our children way up over our heads and pose for pictures. My friend firmly believes that the apples at the top of the tree taste better, because they absorb more sunlight, and I believe him, too, because he is a doctor. And if you can't believe a doctor, who *can* you believe? So we spend a lot of time holding our kids over our heads and waiting for them to pick apples, which takes a long time, because these are small children we're talking about, and they need at least two hands and all of their weight to pluck an apple from a tree, and they don't always have two hands available, because they're usually eating another apple. So we Tatties are waiting and sweating and trembling and smiling for pictures and wondering what exactly is taking them so long, and BONK! Because our kids are not that great at holding onto the apples after they pluck them, either.

(SIDE NOTE: I'm not entirely sure that my friend actually *is* a doctor, because I generally eat a lot of apples when we go to the orchard, and at the end of the day he's still there.)

But at least we pick a good time of the year to go; namely, before Rosh Hashanah. Most people who go apple picking elect to do so on Chol Hamoed, which means that they have only the last days of Yom Tov to finish their apples, and they have to get even more creative in getting rid of them. You can always tell who these people are; they're the ones giving out apples in shul on Simchas Torah. One guy is giving out lollypops, another guy is giving out potato chips, and they're like, "Here's your apple. Don't forget your napkin."

Nevertheless, I think that next year, just for spontaneity's sake, we should take our kids to a honey farm. I figure, once we're bringing along a doctor anyway.

The general mood at Kosherfest is that everyone feels like they're on display.

And as a matter of fact, they *are* on display. Kosherfest is an annual trade show at which thousands of people in the kosher food industry gather to set up booths and feed each other product samples. Basically, it's like a big kiddush, except that everyone is allowed to talk business, because it's not Shabbos. Also, you run into people that you had no idea were even *in* the food industry, and you get to catch up. "What brings you here?" "I'm from the *chassan's* side."

On Display

But I wasn't there from the *chassan's* side. I was there as press. That's what my badge said: "Press." Nobody pressed it. Lucky for me, because there was a pin on the back.

Kosherfest has always been a tremendous boon for the kosher food industry. For the sake of illustration, let's say that you own a huge company that manufactures cheese. You have hundreds of employees, and you're doing very well for yourself, except that you are getting a little sick of your underlings always calling you the "Big Cheese". Now let's say that, as a result of a serious refrigerator malfunction, you suddenly find yourself with about eighty tons of cheese that has turned blue in some places. Your natural response is to find someone to fire, but then your marketing guy informs you that what you have on your hands is actually called "blue cheese", and that people will pay big bucks for it, especially if you pretend you did it on purpose. So you give your cheese a catchy product name, like "Back of the Fridge," and you come to Kosherfest and set up a booth that includes little sample chunks of some of your better sellers, as well as a large tray of your "new product" that is giving off a stench that's interfering with the smoke detectors. And then some fancy restaurant owner walks by, and you can tell that it's a really fancy restaurant because his first reaction is, "Wow! Kosher blue cheese!" And so you sit down with him and try to strike up some kind of distribution deal over the noise of the general buzz of the room and the occasional regular, non-fancy person walking by and going, "Whoa! What's that smell?"

Now I don't want to sound like an uncultured person (I *am* an uncultured person, but I don't want to sound like one, for professional reasons), but I am not a big fan of smelly cheese. My feeling is that if Hashem had wanted us to eat blue cheese, He would have created blue milk. But I did try a piece, purely for the purpose of journalism, and I ended up running straight over to the Kedem booth.

That is not to say that all the food there was bad. In fact, most of it was good. But you could tell when the manufacturers knew that they had a good product, and when they weren't so sure about it but were hoping to sell some anyway. The ones who knew that their food was good, such as the booth that was giving out buffalo wings and lamb schwarma, just put the food out and watched quietly while everyone enjoyed it. Kind of like your Bubby does. The ones with iffy food, meanwhile, felt like they had to spend the entire time while you were chewing describing the benefits of the food – health benefits, allergy benefits, whatever. No one felt the need to explain the benefits of the buffalo wings. Or else they explain how they came up with the product, and you have to stand there with your mouth full and pretend that you like it.

"Do you like it?" they say. "It's not really cheese."

"Mmmo?" you ask.

"It's not," they say. "We don't even know *what* it is. We found it in our basement. We think it's from that time that we tried to make Havdalah candles. But it's cheesy, huh?"

"Mm-hmm," you say, thinking that this is definitely what Yehudis should have used in the Chanukah story.

Also, some of the companies brought along products that didn't really translate very well into samples. I was walking down one of the aisles, looking to see if anyone was handing out coffee samples, when someone handed me a small plastic cup containing about an ounce of barbecue sauce and a pretzel. So I wanted to know:

On Display

Were they selling the pretzels or the barbecue sauce? Or were they selling the little plastic cups? "Look, it can hold an ounce of barbecue sauce AND a pretzel!" I figured that they were probably selling sauce, because if they were selling pretzels, they weren't doing a very good job selling it by implying that they were only really good with barbecue sauce. But at least this was better than some of the other sauce companies, who just handed people a small cup and a spoon.

It turned out that they were, in fact, selling the sauce, and the woman there explained that their company was run out of Seattle by her husband, who was trying to fund his *kollel*. (He opened a *kollel* AND invented a barbecue sauce. That's called living the American dream.)

(He also gets to send his wife across the country to market it.)

In fact, a lot of booth owners tried to tell me their stories, because when they saw my badge, they thought I was actual press, and they suddenly had visions of major write-ups in newspapers that would net them millions of dollars. So I had to keep explaining to people that I'm a humor columnist, and then watch it slowly dawn on them that the more time they spent talking to me, the more of a chance there was that I would make irreverent jokes about them in print.

So I didn't get a whole lot of interviews. But I did get to notice things like market trends. For instance, the current market trend seems to be to sell foods that aren't really the foods that they're supposed to be, for people who want to *think* that they're eating those foods but don't *actually* want to eat them, but don't want to eat the replacement foods either unless they look like the foods that they want to think that they're eating. Over the course of the day, I saw wheat-free bread, gluten-free noodles (made from corn), veggie chips (their slogan was, "Made from the Goodness of Beans"), peanut-free peanut butter, pareve cheesecake, dairy-free cheese, fish-free sushi, caffeine-free tea, and crabless crab cakes, which to my understanding is just cake. I like cake. But that did *not* taste like cake.

The trend for these kinds of foods follows the alarming discovery by the scientific community that almost everything can kill you. Except for soy, apparently. But luckily, soy can be made to taste like anything, kind of like the manna in the desert. In fact, most of the above-mentioned foods were made from soy. (The fish-free sushi was one of the exceptions -- it was made from marzipan. Seriously.) One such item, which I tasted in between shots of barbecue sauce, was fake peanut butter made from soy. The company's slogan, and I heard them telling this to at least three people, was: "It's Close Enough." (As in, "Mmm! Close enough!") They also had a chunky style of it, and I was almost afraid to ask: "Chunks of what?" "Chunks of roasted soy," the guy said, like that was the most normal thing in the world.

I should have introduced him to the fake cheese people.

Taking it With You

The following columns are all about money, because it turns out there *is* humor in being broke, so long as everyone you know is broke *with* you.

I wrote the first column in this section, "Cheaper Living", in an attempt to get my readers involved. I figured that we, as Jews, are very attached to our money, right? (At least that's the stereotype. Really I think *everyone* likes money, but Jews have just figured out how not to spend it all in one place, unless that place is their kids' school.) So I wrote a column about the different things that I think are a waste of money, and then suggested that my readers write in with their own money-saving ideas, and in the end, almost no one wrote in. Seriously. More people wrote to me when they thought my name might not be Mordechai Schmutter. So I think it was one of four things:

- I seriously misjudged the stereotype, and it turns out that we as Jews are more concerned about the real names of our humor writers than we are about money.

- As a people, we were seriously offended by an article about saving money, and decided to specifically *not* write in.

- People were thrown by the fact that this was the one week that my contact information was left out at the bottom of the article. Or,

- Postage was too expensive.

Cheaper Living

I don't think of myself as cheap. Actually, no one thinks of himself as cheap. Everyone, in his own mind, is a sensible spender, and feels that people who spend less than him are cheap, and people who spend more than him are throwing their money away. But it's all objective, really. Let's say that Person A washes his plastic cutlery after he uses it and puts it back in the drawer for the next time he has guests, while Person B thinks that Person A is crazy. Who is to say who's correct?

I am. Person B is correct. Washing plastic cutlery *is* crazy. I also think it's crazy to save empty tissue boxes so you can fill them with pens that you are afraid to throw away because even though many of them have long since died, maybe when Mashiach comes they'll all spring back to life, and thanks to you there will be enough pens to go around. I also think it's crazy to wait until your kids grow out of their pants and then to cut them into shorts to get one more summer out of them, so that your kids are wearing a pair of shorts which has pockets large enough to hold their pens. I think it's crazy to save seven empty, plastic, one-gallon milk containers for powdered drink mix when your refrigerator can't even hold seven one-gallon milk containers at once. But I don't judge people who do these things, because it is unfair to judge people unless you have walked a mile in their shoes and then looked down and realized that the shoes are actually made from recycled watermelon rinds. Then you can judge them. But it's a lot easier to judge people who spend *more* than you do.

So here is a list of items that, when given a choice, I would usually go for the cheaper one, either because the more expensive one isn't worth the extra money, or because the cheaper one is actively better, or because someone else is paying and I don't want to make waves:

- **Brand-Name Clothing:** What I don't understand is why you would pay good money to have a designer's name printed right on your clothing if the designer himself would set his servants on you if you tried to come into his home and print your name on *his* clothing. And do you really need to specifically buy crocs that have little alligators on the sides?

- **Gas:** Every single gas station on the planet is selling gas for a different price, and no one really knows why. All they know is that the gas in New Jersey is cheaper, and that the attendants pump it for you. And why do they have to pump it for you? Probably because they KNOW that they're much cheaper than all of the other states, and they don't want people sneaking away more gas than they need in plastic milk containers. Nevertheless, some people specifically go to the more expensive gas stations, like they have better gas or something. Maybe these people go for the ambiance, or because their specific gas station sells *cholent*.

- **Restaurants:** Unless the only other choice is an actively bad restaurant where the waiters have to wash their hands before going back outside, you usually don't get what you pay for with really fancy restaurants. The lighting is bad, it takes forever for the food to come, and when it does come, it's a tiny little dollop of something that you weren't even sure of what it was when you ordered it, because it was written on the menu in another language, and you couldn't understand the helpful translation either because it contained words like "broached", and you could barely read it in the first place because the lighting was bad. And the can of Coke that you order with the meal is somehow more expensive than the can of Coke that you get at a pizza shop, even though it's the same Coke. Plus, the waiter is always on top of you. "Have you made your selection yet?" "No, we're still trying to read the menu. Can you please bring us another candle for the middle of the table? And what on Earth are *shallots*?" If they need their menus back so badly, why don't they just print more? The *Chinese* place gives them away for free! It's like they printed up like five menus for the entire restaurant. "Yeah, there are thirty tables, so five menus sounds about right. We can make everyone share."

- **Hotels:** As long as the hotel you're staying in isn't a total hole in the wall, most of the cheaper ones are okay, so long as your expectations aren't too high. So long as things are clean, and the bed is good enough so that your head isn't lower than your feet and there don't appear to be springs trying to escape out of the middle of the mattress, then unless you pay significantly more money, you get the same two beds and a tiny table and a coffeemaker that makes two cups of hot water, depending on how you define a cup, and a set of drawers that you're not going to use because you're already living out of a suitcase, and a small bar of soap that does not appear to actually be made out of soap.

- **Cell Phones:** Every company charges a different amount of money for their cell phone service, and the truth is that they're all about the same. They all conk out when you don't want them to, they all have a million features that you're never going to figure out how to use, and they all make you feel like you're not talking loud enough, especially in public. You can't hear the other person properly, and you think you can fix the problem by talking louder. Maybe you're hoping that he'll get the message and talk louder also, but usually he does not. And they all have embarrassing ring tones. And while, say, Sprint service doesn't work in your living room, the truth is that Nextel doesn't work in your dining room, and T-Mobile doesn't work on your roof. This has nothing to do with your specific carrier; it is actually a ploy by all of the phone companies, which is why they ask you for your home phone number when you purchase a cell phone. Why do they need your home phone number? In case they need to call you? You have a cell phone! So the truth is that they are actually trying to pinpoint where you live, so that they can give you a phone that doesn't work properly in your own house, and you therefore have to spring for a home phone line, too, which you would otherwise not even need because you never take off your earpiece thingy, even during *davening*. Although I'm pretty sure Hashem can hear you without it.

I'm out of room here, thank goodness, but I'm sure that there are items and services for which you too would rather get away with the cheaper one, and I really want to hear what those are. Please write in, and I will try to include them in a future article (along with your name, unless you indicate otherwise). On the other hand, if you are the type of person who does not have any such feelings and would rather judge me and call me a cheapskate, that's fine with me, because I happen to think you're too liberal with your money anyway. But if you send me some, I can maybe write you a fancier column next time.

Even Cheaper Living

A number of weeks ago, I wrote a column about frivolous spending, in which I suggested that readers send me their ideas about products and services on which they were opposed to spending extra money, or, if they were not opposed to spending extra money, to just send me some money instead. For some reason, I did not get nearly as big a reader response as I'd hoped, especially in the way of cash. I didn't get a large response from the people *opposed* to spending money either, but for that I blame the postal hike. At forty-one cents a letter, you can't just go writing to every humor columnist who asks.

So I blame the postal system, mainly because I can't really blame my editors. It's tough to be an editor, what with all of the responsibilities involved. The newspaper I write for is a daily, so every single day the editors have to assign articles to a hundred different writers, spend most of the day offering them helpful writing tips, such as, "WHERE IS THAT ARTICLE ALREADY?", and then they have to collect the articles and send them to a *mashgiach*, who makes sure there is no objectionable content and seals them in heavy plastic, and then the editors have to get all of the remaining words to fit exactly onto the pages, using power tools if necessary, and then they have to put the paper to bed, and say Shema, and hope everything goes alright because they have to start the whole process again bright and early the next day, which actually begins in twenty minutes. So they don't always have time to read all the way through every article to the part where the writer very clearly asks the readers to write in. And if it's getting late, and the little blurb of contact information doesn't want to fit on the bottom of the page, then instead of fighting with it, the editors are just going to leave it out and see if maybe today is the day they actually get to go to sleep. (Or else they're going to cut out part of the article to make it fit.) But originally, I *was* going to blame the editors, on the theory that they're not going to read this far into the article anyway.

Anyway, if you recall, I previously wrote about items that I feel are a total waste of money, such as the fancy, dimly-lit restaurants, what with the waiters looking down their noses at you for mispronouncing the items on the menu, or for bringing a flashlight to read it, or for asking, "That's it? That's the whole steak?" And yet at the same time they're constantly on top of you, asking if you're done with your menus so the other tables can use them, or if you're done with your three-dollar can of coke that they brought you forty-five minutes before the rest of the food, or if you're finished eating your tiny steak already so they can set the table for the next party.

It reminds me of the time I was at a wedding, and I wanted soda, but there was only one glass in front of my plate, and it came pre-filled with water. So I figured that I'd drink all of the water, and then refill the cup with soda. But every time I drank about half the glass, a waiter would sneak up behind me and fill it right back up to the top. So I'd drink some more, and there he was again, refilling my water. "No-no-no-wait!" I'd sputter, between bites of soup, but he didn't listen. It was like he had some kind of water quota, because the caterer came with a certain amount and didn't want to have to bring home the leftovers. Eventually, I somehow managed to down all the water and fill my glass with Sprite. And then, as soon as I was halfway finished my Sprite, the waiter came back and poured in half a cup of water.

I did get *some* responses, though. One woman wrote in to tell me that she doesn't like spending money on garbage bags. I'm not talking about kitchen bags. Kitchen bags are okay, so long as you periodically press everything down so that it is condensed into a heavy wad that rips the garbage bag when you lift it, so that you get some sort of hybrid mixture of everything you've eaten that week on the bottom of your pants leg. I'm talking about *small* garbage bags; the kind that you put in the bin in your bathroom or laundry room. You go to the store and buy a case of sixty bags, and you carry them home in a shopping bag that the store gives you for free. Then, when you get home, you take the garbage bags out of the shopping bag, and you put the shopping bag into one of the garbage bags. But here's a thought: How about we just use the shopping bags as garbage bags? It's too bad that they only give them to you if you actually buy something. I would like to be able to walk into the store and count out fifty shopping bags right in front of the cashier, and then put them on the conveyor belt and ask, "How much?"

Another person mentioned that he doesn't understand why people spend an upwards of sixty dollars on a haircut. And neither do I, because my hair grows alarmingly fast. Every time my father sees me, he tells me to get a haircut, even if I'd just gotten one that morning. This is in contrast to my son, who will be four in February, and whose hair grows so slowly that he has so far in his life only gotten two haircuts. And he didn't even really need the first one; we just gave it to him because he was three, and that is the tradition, whether he needs one or not. Sure, if your job requires you to meet with people who will be less than impressed if you showed up with rows on your head that look like your lawn does after you mow it, then you can go ahead with the expensive haircuts. You can also get a nice haircut if it's your wedding day, never mind that you're going to be wearing a hat. But otherwise I would say to just go with the ten-dollar cuts, or those homemade ones where one of your relatives goes back and forth and back and forth over your head, cutting a little more off each side to make things even, so that by the time you're done you can turn your head sideways and stick it through a mail slot.

Another reader was very annoyed by people who pierce their babies' ears and buy them real earrings. The babies don't want it. They don't care about anything in the world that they can't put into their mouths. So their parents are doing it to make *themselves* feel better. But why? Are you saying that Hashem didn't make your baby cute enough? Who are you dressing your baby up for? Does she have a job interview?

My point is that everyone could think of *something* that he feels is a waste of money, and I urge you to share yours, because I have gone out on a limb twice now, flaunting my spending habits, at the risk of being called cheap. And just in case the editors decide that there is no room for a bio this week, I am even going to stick my contact information into the actual article. You can write to me at Hamodia, 207 Foster Avenue, Brooklyn, NY 11230, or you ca

Mordechai Schmutter is a freelance writer/editor and a humor columnist for Hamodia. You can contact him c/o Hamodia Magazine, 207 Foster Avenue, Brooklyn, NY 11230, or you can email him at magazine@hamodia.com.

Today's "Clueless Homeowner" topic is: Winterizing Your Home.

Most people don't think about winterizing their homes until they begin taking down their sukkahs and wondering why on Earth they didn't stop to consider, back when they were actually *buying* their sukkahs, where they were going to store them for the rest of the year. Heavy wooden panels are a great idea until you have to drag them up three flights to your attic.

But winterizing is very important, especially these days, with gas prices achieving new spiritual heights all the time. It got to the point where people had to carpool to the gas station. So when you stop to think about how much fuel it takes to heat your home, and how you got gas bills last winter that caused you to turn the heat off and put on all of your clothes at once so that in your Chanukah pictures you looked like you went a little overboard with the latkes, and about the fact that warm air is constantly escaping from your home during the winter and cold air is escaping during the summer, then you have to wonder why you aren't smart enough to pick yourself up and get out of the house before you die of oxygen deprivation.

In the old days people didn't have to winterize, because back then they didn't use gas heat. In those days, everyone had fireplaces, which ran on firewood, whose prices were not directly affected by violence in Iraq, unless one actually lived there. In fact, you can easily make a fireplace in your own home by making a base in the middle of your living room out of something that will not catch fire easily, such as bricks or *chametz*, and then making a hole in the ceiling directly above it for ventilation, so long as your upstairs neighbors do not mind. Another option, if you want to save on gas but are not much in the manual dexterity department, is to run out and buy a bunch of space heaters, which run on electricity. Space heaters tend to work very well, barring the occasional third-degree burn, until the power runs out during a snowstorm, at which point you're going to have to invest in a generator, which runs on gas. So you really can't win.

That is why you need to winterize, if you can figure out how. Most home-repair books contain a section on winterizing your home, but they are written for people who already know the basics of home construction and use terms like "parameter" and "joist" in everyday language, as in, "I think we have to joist this thing about three parameters to the left." For the rest of us, these books read like those old-fashioned English Gemaras we used to study from, the ones that must have been primarily designed to boost our vocabularies, because most of the time we had no idea what they were saying. "Is-ku-fa? What's that? Let's check the English. Hmm... Okay, what's a veranda? We're going to need a dictionary." Luckily, *our* instructions for winterizing are written in plain English, so the only real drawback is that we very obviously have no idea what we're talking about.

- **WEATHER STRIPPING --** One of the biggest causes of heat loss in your home is those little cracks around your windows and doors. To conduct an experiment, walk over to your front window and wave your hand around the edges. Do you feel that rush of cold air coming in? Now look out the window at the passerby who thinks you were waving at him. Look, he's waving back. You can smile and wave again, or you can give him the international sign for "I wasn't waving at you; I was just checking for drafts," which basically consists of a whole lot more waving and shaking your head. It's up to you.

    Next, go to your local home repair store and purchase some weather stripping. Your two basic choices, when it comes to weather stripping, are adhesive and non-adhesive. There is really no difference between the two, except that adhesive stripping is going to get all tangled up and stick to your fingers and then lose all of its stickiness, and you'll spend the rest of the season with a massive string dragging behind as you open and close your doors.

- You're also going to have to guess exactly how wide each length of stripping needs to be, because there are hundreds of choices, most of which appear to be the same exact size, except that whoever labeled the packages seems convinced that they are not. One option would be to uninstall all of your windows and doors and bring them into the store, and then to try to convince the cashier that you really did bring them into the store with you, all the while praying that no one on your block decides to make the most of the fact that you just removed all of your windows and doors and drove away.

- **CAULKING** – Any cracks on the outside of your house are going to have to be covered with caulking. Caulking is a weird gluey substance that comes in big tubes, like cake frosting, and which oozes out of the caulking gun all over your shoes, because once you cut that tube open there is no way to stop it from leaking until it's empty. So you're going to have to work fast, get all of your tools, ladders, etc. ready ahead of time, and not let anything distract you. While you're working, you may have some neighbors come by and offer helpfully insightful comments, such as, "Hey! Look who's caulking! Ha ha!" A nice piece of weather stripping over their mouths should take care of the problem.

  (**CAUTION:** After using your caulking gun, make sure to store it in a safe place, and, if you have children, to hide your caulk in a separate room, preferably in someone else's house entirely. More and more children are admitted into the hospital every day with caulk-related injuries. Most of these children have older brothers.)

- **INSULATION** – If you can, poke around in your attic to make sure that you have adequate insulation. One of the best types of insulation is fiberglass insulation, so if you keep a fiberglass sukkah up there you should be okay. In addition, you're going to want to add insulation anywhere that you can. When my wife and I first moved into our current house, we noticed that there was a six-inch gap under our front door that had absolutely no insulation, and that, as a result, our living room was always cold. So my mother-in-law showed up at our house with a couple of nerdy fleece vests that she said would save us on heating costs. As soon as she left, we stuffed those vests into the gap, and since then we've saved hundreds of dollars.

- **HOT WATER HEATERS** – If you want to use less fuel to heat the water in your home, you can use a hot-water heater blanket, which looks sort of like those little hats that covered the toilet paper in your grandparents' house. That's a lot of knitting, but you can do it in front of your fireplace.

- **FIREPLACES** – Make sure to plug up your fireplace for the winter, because they leak air like crazy. It's a big hole in your roof. What were you thinking?

- **THAT LAST DRAFTY ROOM** – No matter how much you strip and caulk and insulate and plug, there will be one room in the house that will always feel cold and drafty. There is no scientific reason for this. We suggest you check your *mezuzos*.

We hope these instructions are of some help in keeping you warm for the winter. If they are not, and your house is cold and everyone gets sick, it's still nothing to fret about. At least you have your health. But if you think that's bad, wait until my mother-in-law finds out how we've been using her vests.

Promising the Moon

Ever since the dawn of civilization, mankind has been obsessed with real estate. When Columbus got to the New World, the first question he asked the Native Americans was, "How much for these Bahamas?" (Actually, that was more like his third question. His first question was, "Where can I lie down?" and his second questions was, "Why do you guys call yourselves Native Americans when this is clearly the East Indies?") In fact, most of the major wars throughout history can be attributed to real estate. So when mankind first took a giant leap on the moon, the one question running through everyone's mind was, "Where can we lie down?"

Real estate has always been about finding a good place to lie down.

It seems that recently, many people have been trying to lie down on the moon. In fact, a number of companies are now selling actual properties up there to private individuals – since we are talking about the moon, we will call them "lunatics" (this is not a disrespectful term, just a lunar one) – who like the idea of owning property that can be seen only with a telescope. It's kind of like adopting a highway, but it's easier to keep clean, because, aside from astronauts occasionally walking up and planting flags on your lawn, there's not much littering up there. But before you start thinking that this sounds too much like a Country Yossi song (not the one about the *cholent*; the other one), the obvious question springs to mind: Considering that these companies are merely real-estate firms, just whom is everyone buying these properties *from*?

The answer to that question is a man by the name of Dennis Hope. In 1967, as the result of major international confusion, the United Nations put together an Outer Space Treaty, the basic gist of which was that everyone was launching people up into space with flags, and the last thing that we needed was major international confusion up there, too. So the treaty states, using heavy legal jargon, that the moon and all other celestial bodies cannot be claimed by any country that has signed the treaty, as well as any country that didn't have to sign the treaty because they could not produce an automobile that could make it all the way across a parking lot without pooping out, let alone a working spaceship.

But then, in 1980, Dennis Hope finally read all of the way through the treaty – he was the first person to do so – and he noticed that, while the treaty banned *governments* from owning celestial bodies, it said nothing about private individuals. Dennis also noticed that, according to American law, it is absolutely legal to put your name on any property that does not have an owner, or is owned by Native Americans. So he marched right down to wherever it is you march down to for these things and registered the moon in his name. But recently Dennis has decided, out of the goodness of his heart, to share the moon with others, provided that others are willing to share their money with him. He also has various bridges for sale, if you're interested.

As Dennis's claim has never been legally contested (in the same way that you never legally contest an ant who claims your sandwich on the basis that no other ant has registered for it), the moon retailers are providing buyers with both a photo of their property, as seen from a distance, as well as an official piece of paper saying that they own a piece of the moon. As one of the retailers, called "Lunar Land Owner", says in their ad, the certificate makes for a great conversation piece. We can just picture one of those conversations now:

HUSBAND: "Ta-daa! Happy anniversary!"

WIFE: "It's a piece of paper."

HUSBAND: "No, you have to *read* the piece of paper."

WIFE: "I did. Is this what you did with our money? We needed that money for wall treatments!"

HUSBAND: "Don't worry, we can hang up the certificate! Hey, where are you going?"

But all of this is already causing problems for NASA. In 1997, three men in Yemen sued them for landing on Mars, which they said was their property. Also, in 2001, a company called Orbital Development sent NASA an invoice for landing a probe on 433 Eros (an asteroid between Mars and Jupiter), and NASA is *still* fighting that one in court. It turns out that there's no point in owning property that you can't visit if you can't hassle NASA about it once in a while. So we think that at some point, someone high up is going to try reading through that Outer Space Treaty again.

Nevertheless, after seven years and fifty-six million acres of moon space, the one country that has given Dennis the greatest amount of business is, of course, Israel. Israeli citizens have bought a tenth of the property sold, at two hundred-fifty shekel per five hundred square meters of land, plus shipping and handling. Sure, it's solid rock, but that's what the Native Americans said about Manhattan, and then they sold it for twenty-four dollars worth of fake jewelry. (That's a *lot* of fake jewelry.)

The Israelis are buying these properties through a company called Crazyshop, which offers unique gifts, including the right to name an actual star after a loved one (unless your loved one's name is "Pluto"). So chances are pretty good that there's a star out there named Shprintzy. Buyers of these stars also get a photo and a map, but if you ask me, it's entirely possible that they're really just selling everyone the same star over and over. *I* would. The only star that anyone can really recognize, based on a map, is the actual sun, and some old guy named Sol already got to that one. Crazyshop also has a deal wherein you can buy a "Galactic Package" consisting of both a star *and* a spot on the moon.

HUSBAND: "But wait! Come back! It was part of a package!"

So why are Israelis so interested in owning moon properties? Many of them say they want it for their grandchildren, which I think is great. *My* grandmother usually bought me sweaters.

This is coming off a recent announcement that NASA is planning on building an International Base Camp at the South

Pole. Of the moon. Really. This is because the poles are the only parts of the moon that don't wind up in the dark for half the month. So maybe these people are just buying land as an investment, so that they can haggle with NASA for it later. Or maybe they actually want to live on it, and write long *sefarim* about how to accomplish various *mitzvos* on the moon, such as *kiddush hachodesh*. At the beginning of every month, every Jew on the moon would have to look down and begin a mad dash toward *beis din*, gravity permitting.

Or maybe all of these Israelis buying up pieces of the moon are a part of a bigger plan. Maybe they are doing this so that, when the Arabs find out about it, the Arabs will all load up their WMDs with fuel and fly up there and claim that the moon is theirs, and that it *has* been for centuries. Let them try to suicide bomb each other in a total vacuum. Or they can open up casinos. No one really cares.

Gastronomical

When summertime rolls around each year, it becomes time to load up the family car with all of your belongings and then see if you can push it all the way to the bungalow colony. You'd have to, considering the price of gas these days.

Gas prices have been rising alarmingly these past few years, mostly without explanation. Why *are* gas prices rising, anyway? Any time we are given a reason, when the reason goes away, the prices still stay up. It seems as if no one actually knows what's causing it at all. We keep reading in the news about how officials are flying all over the country to put their heads together and figure this thing out. This begs the question: Why are they flying to energy

Gastronomical

conferences? Shouldn't they walk? At least set up a conference call or something.

So, in the interest of writing a well-informed article, I have done a lot of research on this topic, and I have found literally dozens of theories, most of which involve economics. But if I had any vague understanding of economics, I would not have become a humor writer. One theory, for example, has a lot to do with supply and demand, and the fact that there is now an increased demand for oil due to our driving around in big machines that are designed to climb up mountains, but that we use mainly to get to the supermarket. Another theory says that supply has gone up, too, thanks to technology, but that we now have an increased demand thanks to the war in Iraq, which, whether or not it is a good idea (and there is no way I'm going down *that* road), is using a scary amount of gas. Also, some people blame price gauging, because somehow the price of heating oil goes up in the winter, and the price of car fuel goes up in the summer, which all seems very convenient if you ask them. And it's not like we can just stock up on the off-season. And another theory, of course, has to do with tension in the Middle East, because no business in the world is governed by tension as much as the gasoline industry.

But no one really knows the reason. When the King of Saudi Arabia died, speculators said that prices would go up, and they did, despite the fact that his son had been running things for quite some time before. And when Hurricane Rita was on the horizon, speculators once again said that gas prices would go up, and they did. Come to think of it, I think the problem is the speculators. Maybe we should do something about *them*. Send them over to Iraq if they're so good at predicting things. "I speculate that we're going to get attacked from the left."

But never mind all of this finger-pointing; the main question is, what do we actually *do* about the rising gas prices? And what are our so-called scientists doing about it? Nothing. They're still trying to figure out whether Pluto is a planet. Not that it matters. It's not like they're ever going to get up there anyway, with gas prices the way they are.

But actually, some scientists say they've come out with something called an MPG cap, which I found out from a friend of mine named Yitzchak Stern, although not really, because I seldom use real names. Yitzchak has become part of a "pyramid business situation" wherein he tries to convince his family and friends to buy MPG caps, and they look at him like he's inviting them to join a cult.

As it turns out, the MPG cap is a small capsule that looks like a vitamin pill that you feed your car through the gas tank every time you fill up, and it's supposed to be 100% organic and help the car run more efficiently. The scientists looked at people taking vitamins, and they asked themselves, "Why can't cars do the same thing?" This is why people like you and me are not scientists.

Now I'm not disputing the logic of giving your car a pill. Sometimes you feel like your car may have a headache from some of the bass-heavy music you've been playing within its head, and you think some Advil may help. Or sometimes your car is making funny noises, and you really think it can benefit from Alka-Seltzer. But you can't just go around stuffing random things into your gas tank without knowing what they are.

In order to understand how the MPG cap works, we must first understand how a car operates in the first place. Most of us have long chosen not to think about how our cars work, because from

Gastronomical

what we've heard it involves thousands of tiny explosions right under our hoods, and what if just one of those explosions was not as tiny as the others? That would explain potholes.

But the way it works is that the gas is fed, in tiny increments, into the engine, which is a big, filth-encrusted hulk that you'd see if you ever managed to figure out how to pop your hood. Inside the engine are little hollow cylinders, and each one contains a piston, which can move in and out of the cylinder as needed. The gas is let into the cylinder, where it explodes, forcing the piston to come flying out of the cylinder, except that then it has to come right back in, because it's attached by gears, the poor piston. And then the whole process repeats itself. That's what turns the wheels of your car. I'm not sure how power steering works.

The problem is that not all of the energy of the explosion goes into firing the piston. Some of it escapes through the cracks, and some of it gets absorbed into the walls of the engine. Energy is like that – it's always trying to escape when you don't want it to. (It has too much energy, if you ask me.) So what the caps do is create a micro-thin coating so that nothing can get out, but you have to keep adding more coating, because you keep blowing it up.

I don't know for sure whether these pills actually work, because I have never personally used them, and neither has Yitzchak, who told me that he still has them in his car. I think this is because we live in New Jersey, where it is illegal to pump your own gas, and he's afraid that if he hands a pill to the attendant and tells him to put it in the tank, the guy will laugh so hard that he'll get gas on his shoes.

So what do we do in the meantime? Here are some expert-suggested tips to save on gas:

A CLEVER TITLE GOES HERE

- Whenever possible, try to carpool. In fact, you'll notice that whenever astronauts go into outer space, they carpool.

- Don't carry around extra weight. For every hundred pounds in your car, you get almost one mile less per gallon. See if you can mention this to the people in your carpool without coming straight out and saying that they weigh too much.

- When possible, use air vents instead of windows. Windows create a drag, and it's like driving around with a big sail behind you. The perfect car would have rear windows that roll down, but then the Jewish people as a whole would lose a lot of yarmulkes.

- Use momentum to your advantage. When you come to the top of a hill, just coast down, traffic permitting of course. If you really want to have fun while doing this, you can put your hands up like you're on a roller coaster and yell, "AAAAAAHH!"

- But don't do this while carpooling.

There's No "Nun" In "Yuntiff"

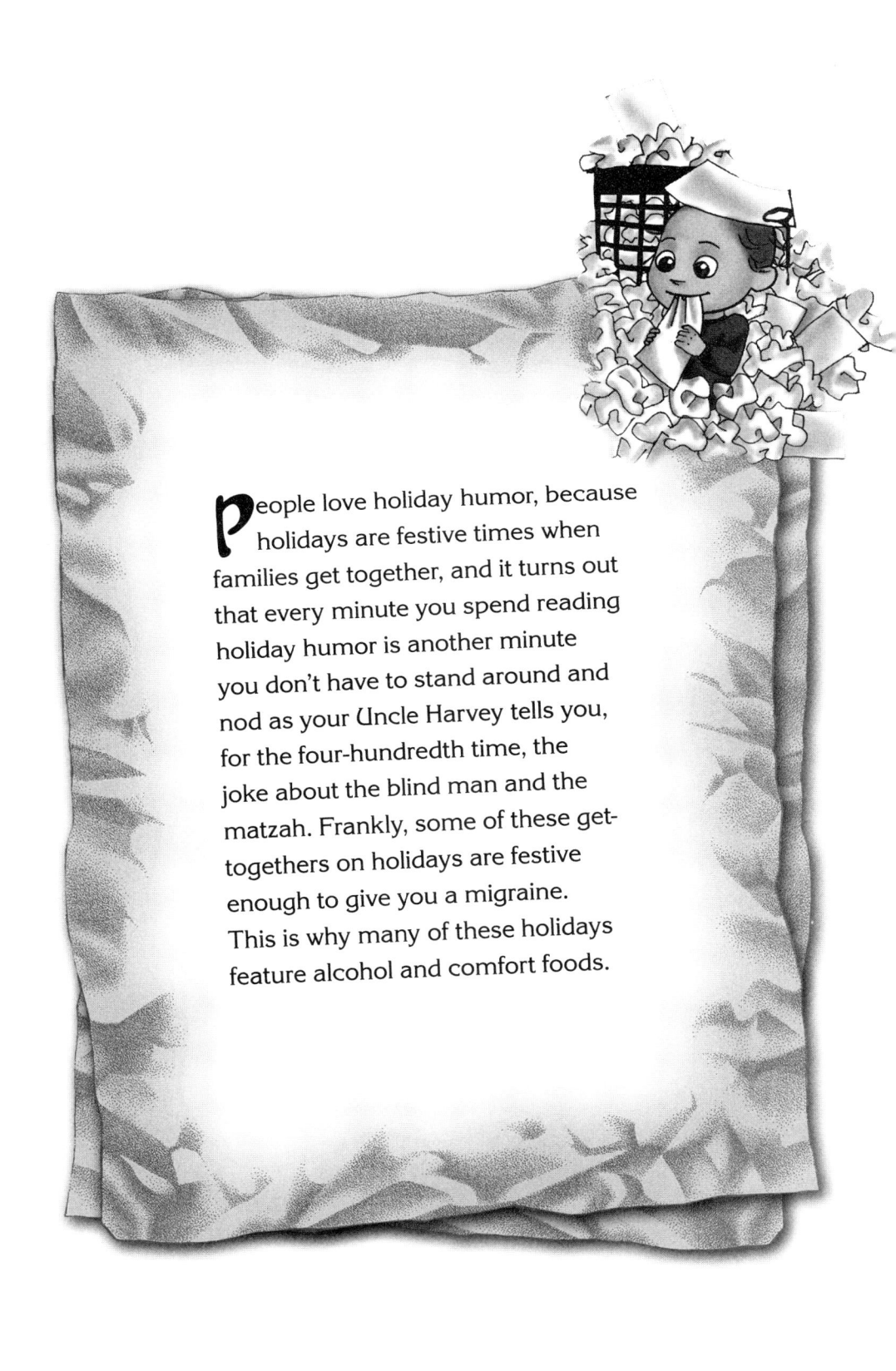

People love holiday humor, because holidays are festive times when families get together, and it turns out that every minute you spend reading holiday humor is another minute you don't have to stand around and nod as your Uncle Harvey tells you, for the four-hundredth time, the joke about the blind man and the matzah. Frankly, some of these get-togethers on holidays are festive enough to give you a migraine. This is why many of these holidays feature alcohol and comfort foods.

Relaxing is Cleaning, Too

I'm going to go out on a limb and say that when you do Pesach cleaning, most of you will not actually have time to read this article. Instead, you will be in the middle of a massive cleaning spree, and because you can't break an omelet without making some eggs, you'll have categorized absolutely everything you own into little piles in the living room. But then you will need to rest up from the mess you made, and will find a couple of seconds to curl up with something to read, and the excuse you'll have prepared, if anyone asks, is that you are weeding down the magazine pile as part of your cleaning process. But you're not fooling anyone. Magazines and books aren't *chametz*.

That said, I have taken the time to compile a series of cleaning tips, based on items from the news, which may help you get rid of the guilt from the fact that you're not cleaning. And that way, when my wife is trying to Pesach clean in our house and she asks me, loudly, if I can come help her search through all of the kids' coat pockets for lollypop sticks, I can say, "Sorry, can't. Putting together a list of cleaning tips."

Our first tip today comes from a recent AP article about a chimpanzee named Judy who got out of her cage at a zoo in Little Rock, Arkansas, after one of the zookeepers opened the door to her cage, not knowing that she was in there. Pardon me for asking, but isn't making sure the animals are in their cages, like, the first thing they teach you in zookeepers' school? If he didn't think she was in her cage, why was he just wandering in? He should have been out looking for her! It's an escaped chimpanzee—who *knows* what it can do!

It turned out that what Judy could do was root around in the fridge of the feeding area, sample a bunch of chimp snacks and some soft drinks, and scrub the facilities with a toilet brush.

While she was at it, Judy also wrung out a sponge and scrubbed down the fridge. She was eventually handed a yogurt that was laced with sedatives, and ended up falling asleep on top of the fridge holding half of a cinnamon raisin loaf. This begs the question: Why would they give her sedatives, seeing as she was doing them a service? How many prison inmates escape their cells to scrub down the little warden's room and eat yogurt? Is there some rule against cleaning the bathrooms at the zoo? Apparently so.

But if there's one lesson that we can take from this story, it's that you should definitely include your children in the cleaning

Relaxing is Cleaning, Too

process, even if they're going to raid the fridge and make more of a mess than what they will clean. All you need is enough sedatives for when they get out of control. And if falling asleep on top of the refrigerator with a cinnamon raisin loaf doesn't say "teenager", I don't know what does.

Our next story today concerns Debbie Phillips of West Virginia, who came home one August day to find that her home had been broken into. But strangely enough, nothing had been taken. Instead, her entire house, top to bottom, had been cleaned. Apparently, Judy gets around.

Debbie immediately called her husband, who denied cleaning the house, and then she called her next-door neighbor, who told her she was crazy. The article does not say why Debbie thought her next-door neighbor did it. Sometimes you give a neighbor a spare key, and you don't know *what* they'll do. (Something to keep in mind if you're selling your own *chametz*.)

So for a while, Debbie didn't know what to think. But sometimes these things happen. A burglar breaks into a house and says to himself, "Wow! I can't find *anything* in this dump!" So he gets out the steel wool and the rubber gloves, and before he knows it, the workday's over and he's too tired to even remember why he came in the first place.

But about a month later, Debbie's son called her at work to say that there was a cleaning woman at the door. As it turns out, her neighbor across the street, with a similar house number, the same number of rooms to be cleaned, and a house key hidden in a similar spot outside, had hired a cleaning service, and the poor woman had come to the wrong door. More than once, apparently.

But as far as lessons we can take away from this, most of you who are reading this story are thinking the same thing: "How can I arrange for this to happen to *me*?" Well, it's not easy, let me tell you. First, you have to find neighbors with similar house numbers, and convince them of the benefits of hiring a cleaning service, without coming right out and saying that you think their house can really use a good cleaning. The more of your neighbors you talk to about this, the better your odds. Then, you have to find out where they hide their keys, or just make a whole bunch of copies of your own key, and scatter them in random places around your yard. Good luck with that, by the way.

But the real lesson we can learn from this is that it always pays to keep your house a bit less than perfectly clean, so that you can tell if someone's been cleaning, and also so that you can at least have some kind of benefit from it. Also, for all you husbands out there, it's okay to lie for *shalom bayis*. So if your wife calls you in a panic and asks if you snuck home in the middle of the day and cleaned your house, then by all means you say, "YES!"

Husbands are not very smart in West Virginia.

Our final story concerns a window washer in Nashville, Tennessee, who fell asleep on a scaffolding twenty stories up. He was spotted by a man named Leroy Anderson, who watched him sleep for about a half-hour before calling the fire department. "Look, honey, there's a man sleeping on a windowsill."

After examining him thoroughly, doctors couldn't determine what made him doze off. Maybe someone gave him yogurt. Or maybe he was trying to get away with sleeping at work, and he figured that it was impossible for his boss to catch him sleeping up there. Imagine his surprise when he woke up to a news chopper and the entire fire department's Kitten Rescue Unit. But I think that if you find your job monotonous enough that you are just dozing off twenty stories above the ground on a piece of wood held aloft by emergency brakes, then maybe it's time for a more exciting job. Zookeeper, for example.

But the lesson here is that you definitely should not overwhelm yourself with cleaning work. I have no doubt that this person was cleaning the windows top to bottom, as window washers often do, and he looked down and saw that he had twenty stories left, and said, "Forget it. I'm taking a nap."

My point is that there's nothing wrong with reading a short article here and there. But I do hope that I've sufficiently distracted you from your task, considering all I really did was talk about cleaning.

Why are you still sitting there?

Food For Thought

The night after Pesach is one of the biggest food shopping nights for Jews, second only to the can-can sale. That said, I really feel bad for the *goyim*. Most years, I am among the first ones into the supermarket, because I want to avoid the crowds as much as possible, and I see all these *goyim* wandering around, like curious little woodland creatures, wondering, "What's with the big piles of flour and noodles in the middle of the store? Is there some kind of marathon coming up?" One of them cautiously approaches a pile and picks up, say, a bottle of ketchup, checks the price again, shrugs, and puts it in his cart. Then I can see him thinking about whether or not to take another bottle of ketchup, as he slowly moseys over to the big mountain of cereal boxes. These poor guys are there on a regular weeknight because they figure they can have the whole store to themselves, but they have no idea what's going to hit them. As I am always looking to stem the spread of anti-Semitism, I want to warn them: "Run! Save yourselves! Forget the cereal; just get to the checkout! No, don't bother browsing the Passover foods; they're going to taste a little off! Yeah, I know they're half price; just leave them! Go!" But that will just make *me* look like a crazy person, and if they do get out of there before the stampede, that's all they're going to be talking about for the rest of the night. "Did you see that Jewish guy? He just chased us out of the store! That was scary."

So I don't say anything, and they quizzically wander over to the mountain of cereal, and then suddenly the ground starts shaking, items start pitching forward off the shelves, and the *goyim* look around, like, "What's going on?" And then, in the span of about ninety seconds, not only is the entire store densely packed to the point that it would take a Rubik's cube expert to get everyone out safely, but somehow, within those ninety seconds, the checkout lines have also filled to the point where any one of them promise a good forty-five-minute wait. How do these people shop so fast? Are they even *buying* anything? Or did they come all the way out just to stand in line so they can get out of putting away their Pesach dishes? So much for beating the crowds.

In fact, as you spend the rest of the night waiting in line, you can see the faces of the *goyim*, still frozen in shock. "What just happened? Why is everyone buying the same five items? The prices aren't even that good!" If they're lucky, some kind-hearted soul will explain to them that there is no major Jewish holiday coming up that calls for flour and cereal and noodles with ketchup, but that we are buying these foods because Passover is over; and that no, the prices are not even that good.

But that's how the stores get us. Once upon a time, they used to advertise real sales. For instance, they would say that, for a given week, zucchini was half off, and everyone would go out and buy a zucchini. Then the next week, they would announce that cucumbers were half off, and everyone would rush out and buy cucumbers. All of this power eventually got to their heads. Nowadays, instead of saying "half off", the circulars say things like, "Buy six zucchinis, and get one free." So now everyone has to buy seven zucchinis, and no one really wants to *eat* seven zucchinis in the limited amount of time before they go bad. But the stores do this because nowadays we are just so bad at math that we only see the word FREE, and we don't stop to think that we are getting a unnatural amount of zucchini for only a seventh off the regular price. But we don't know what a seventh off the regular price is anyway, because it's too hard to figure out. It's like when the circulars say, "Buy 5 for $12.56", and no one has any idea whether that is a good price, but it must be, because otherwise why would they put it in the circular?

But what if it's not a good price? That's how I ended up with nine bottles of *chametz-dik* salad dressing three weeks before Pesach. My wife and I had to invent new things to do with salad dressing:

"What kind of soup are we having?"

"Creamy Italian."

The key to shopping nowadays is that, when the circular says, "Limit four" (or some other arbitrary limit number), it is probably a good price, and the reason they are limiting it is because they are worried about people getting carried away and making off with their entire stock in a rental truck, so that they have to give everyone else rain-checks to the point where they are still handing out the item for below cost price well into the next century.

But the main goal of retailers and manufacturers, it seems, is to keep trying to outsmart the very people who keep them in business. For instance, at some point a lot of companies realized that, instead of charging more for groceries, they could just make the groceries smaller. But they didn't want people to notice this, so they put big labels on their products that said they were "Easier to Pour". Great. A cup of soda is easier to pour from than a bottle is, but I'm not spending ninety-nine cents on a cup of soda. Unless I'm in a restaurant. Then I will, but I don't know why.

Where did this come from? Were people actually writing in?

Dear Manufacturers,

I enjoy your orange juice, but I really wish it were easier to pour. Why don't you try making the bottles skinnier, but not lowering the price at all?

Of course it's easier to pour! It's lighter! I say, instead of devoting their time to making things easier to pour, all of these juice scientists should figure out how to make the bottles so that we can get out the last little drop of juice, considering the cap is now located on the side.

But we can't be too hard on them. Remember how the orange juices *used* to be, with the cardboard spout that no one could open? I spent many happy hours as a child mangling those cartons. But a lot of items can still use work. These days, you have to open everything with your teeth. If you go to the average person's house and look through their cabinets, you will see that it looks like they have vermin. Have you ever tried opening a package of pastrami? And how about those fifty-pound blocks of cheese that come wrapped in bulletproof plastic? I have a huge *milchig* knife that I use for nothing other than opening packages of cheese. That, and cutting bagels. Strangely enough, those are the two biggest causes of kitchen-related injury in my home. My guess is that scientists keep coming up with lists of foods that can kill you, and food manufacturers figure that if you can't open their products, they can't kill you. But the knife can kill you. To this day, I do not remember how I got my knife out of the original packaging. I probably backed over it with my car.

These are just some of the thoughts that go through your head when you're waiting in line on the night after Pesach. Next year, I think I'm going to grow my *own chametz*. The wait will definitely be shorter.

Stop and Smell the Parsley

If you are a man, chances are you know nothing about flowers. Sure, you appreciate them as Hashem's creations, the same way you appreciate a rhinoceros or an ostrich, but chances are that you're not going to bring home a rhinoceros or an ostrich to put on your Yom Tov table. But sometimes you have to buy flowers anyway, and frankly, they scare you. For one thing, they all look pretty much alike. The only ones you can actually recognize by name are roses, and that's because there's a picture of one on your wedding *bentcher*.

It is for this reason that I have put together a beginners' Q & A column about flowers, using questions sent in by actual husbands via telepathy, because they were all too scared to ask me in person. Or else I just made them up.

(AUTHOR'S QUALIFICATION TO WRITE THIS COLUMN: The author has been married for over five years, during which he has bought flowers *more than eight times*. Also, in his single days, he would sometimes get invited out of yeshivah for meals, and he would buy flowers for his hosts, because he *still* doesn't quite look old enough to walk into a liquor store.)

Q: What exactly is the appeal of flowers?

A: Flowers are pretty, and they smell nice, and are relatively inexpensive compared to jewelry, except that jewelry lasts for years and years and eventually gets fought over by your children, whereas flowers sometimes die on the way home from the store.

Q: They seem like a waste of money, don't they? How about I buy something that actually lasts, like another vase?

A: Actually, the fact that flowers die works out in your favor. You'll never hear anyone say, "Let's not get them flowers; they already *have* flowers."

Q: What type of flowers should I buy?

A: In general, if you buy flowers every Friday on the way home from work, you can probably get away with flowers that will last for a couple of days, whereas if you buy flowers once a year, they had better last you at least until the next Shavuos. Or else you can do what I do, which is, go into the flower shop and ask, "What can I get for *X* dollars?" Florists are used to dealing with clueless husbands, and they will cheerfully point you toward a bouquet that does not appear to have any actual flowers on it. That's how you know it's time to up your price range.

Q: What is the difference between buying flowers from a florist and buying them from a street vendor?

A: About thirty-five dollars.

Q: No, I mean a *real* difference.

A: Okay. Street flowers usually last about two days.

Q: *Shavuos* is two days.

A: What are you saying?

Q: How about the planting flowers they have for sale at Home Depot? Can I just buy those? They last longer.

A: Okay. But good luck explaining this to your wife.

Q: I'm not buying the flowers for my wife. I'm buying them for Shavuos.

A: No, you're buying them for your wife. Shavuos or not, you're still going to come home from the store and say, "Look, I brought you flowers!" Single yeshivah guys don't buy flowers for their dorm rooms for Shavuos. At best, they spray around a can of floral-scented air freshener.

Q: How long will my flowers last out of the water?

A: Not very long. Once you buy your flowers, you're going to want to get home as soon as possible. Make irresponsible traffic decisions if you have to. If a cop pulls you over, just explain that you have flowers in the back seat, and then ask if you can please have a police escort to your home.

Q: Really?

A: Really. I remember how one year it was about ninety-five degrees on Erev Shavuos, and I'd had the idea to buy Italian ices for Yom Tov, but I had to make a choice between letting the ices sit in the hot car while I stood in line for flowers, or letting the flowers sit in the car while I ran into the supermarket.

Q: So what did you do?

A: I bought the ices first, and then took them into the flower shop with me, and spent a lot of my waiting time standing casually inside the flower refrigerator and pretending to have a genuine interest in browsing through the flowers, and at the end I just asked them for suggestions anyway.

Q: What do I do with the flowers once I get them home?

A: Every time I buy my wife flowers, she carefully cuts a piece off the bottom of each stem, at an angle, before she puts them in the water. I had no idea you were supposed to do this. I would just plop them in the water, and they would be sitting in the vase haphazardly, with the buds perched about three and a half feet off the table.

Q: Is there any way I can preserve my flowers to make them last longer?

A: There are actually many different techniques, and every woman has her own. Think about how you preserve your *lulav* come Sukkos time. You may keep them in a vase; you may wrap them in tinfoil or wet newspaper and put them in your fridge. On the other hand, if you are the type of guy who shows up to shul on the second day of Sukkos with *aravos* that are brown and scraggly and dropping a trail of leaves from your home to the shul, then you definitely need help preserving your flowers.

Q: I heard that different flowers are supposed to send different messages to the receiver. Is there any truth to this?

A: Yes. In Victorian times, people used flowers to convey secret messages to each other. Some flowers signified friendship or devotion, while others signified hatred or war or even death. "Dear France. We hate you. Have some flowers."

IMPORTANT NOTE TO WOMEN: Nowadays, most of these meanings have fallen by the wayside, so if you ever receive flowers, don't read too much into it, or you may end up starting a war. There is no way your husband knows what any of these flowers mean, and if you start yelling at him for getting you flowers, he will be more confused than he has ever been in his life. "No wonder they were so cheap."

Q: Can you give some examples as to what some of these flowers meant, none of which you are making up, of course?

A: Sure.

Palm leaves (*lulavim*) = victory or success.

Wolf's Bane = misanthropy. In other words, if you sent anyone Wolf's Bane, it meant you disliked people in general.

Betony = surprise. "Surprise! I got you Betony!"

Cactus = endurance. If someone was sick, you would give him a cactus, and it would sit on his nightstand so he'd be afraid to reach for the orange juice.

Oleander = caution. We're guessing they put them into their appliance cartons with their instruction manuals.

Parsley = festivities. In other words, if you found parsley on the side of your plate, it meant you were at a *simchah*.

Q: What if I forget to buy flowers?

A: If you ever forget to buy flowers for a special occasion, don't just buy them after the fact. Part of the point of flowers is to have them on display at the occasion, so that everybody can, in turn, say, "Oh. Flowers." And now it's too late. But you *can* buy apology flowers, though.

Q: What's the difference?

A: About forty dollars.

(**P.S.** Yellow roses mean, "I'm sorry.")

As a rule, the Jews as a people have never been technically ept. In fact, we're just the opposite. We're *in*ept. Yet we're expected, with no formal training whatsoever, to gather up our tools once a year (our tools consist of a hammer, two screwdrivers, and a tape measure) and construct a sukkah that will not fall down as soon as we go inside. So a lot of us find ourselves wandering around the aisles of Home Depot looking for a tiny little metal piece that we do not know the name of, and the only way we know how to describe it is that it's "about this big." What we really need is some kind of instruction manual, even if it's not a particularly *good* one. So here goes:

A CLEVER TITLE GOES HERE

WARNING! READ THIS FIRST! Do not swallow pieces of the sukkah. Do not use sukkah panels to hold garage door open while taking out the rest of the panels. Do not tie loosely to the roof of your car and then drive home with one arm holding it onto the roof, as if you're going to be able to stop it if it really wants to fly off. Do not leave jutting out of the trunk of your car and then make short stops on Ocean Parkway. Do not expose to direct sunlight, rain, sleet, snow, tidal waves, mudslides, the hole in the ozone, or peanut butter. Do not read this warning while sleeping or operating heavy machinery. Beware of paper cuts.

You Will Need:

- 1 hammer, even if it's not the kind of sukkah that generally needs a hammer.
- 1 toolbox, to carry the hammer.
- 1 stepladder.
- 1 burly guy who is willing to hold the ladder steady and does not mind getting yelled at from above.
- 1 sukkah.

Where to Place Your Sukkah:

Your best bet would be outside. A lot of people put it up on their decks, just like our forefathers did in the desert. Another popular option is to build your sukkah in the driveway, and then to park your car on the deck. If you do not have a driveway, you might try building the sukkah on your roof. But if you wake up the next morning to find the sukkah in the kiddie pool, then your roof is slanted, and you should probably just go to the in-laws.

Sukkah Basics

Types of Sukkahs:

There are several different types of sukkahs:

- *The Big Heavy Wooden Sukkah with Splinters and Nails Sticking Out In Random Directions.* This sukkah has been in use ever since we can remember, and is the ideal choice for someone who wants to show off how macho he is by accidentally nailing his thumb to the door. It is so heavy that it will generally not blow away until well after your house does.

- *The Sukkah That Is Supposedly Fiberglass But Has No Fibers And Is Definitely Not Glass.* These sukkahs are made with grooves and protrusions at the ends, so that all you have to do is snap a few panels together and "BOOM!"--the wall falls down. So you're definitely going to need someone to hold the walls upright while you work; ideally someone who does not mind getting yelled at from the other side of a wall.

- *The Sukkah That Is Made By Stretching Sheets of Canvas Between Metal Pipes.* This sukkah has the same basic construction as the Wright Brothers' original airplane or the sail of a ship, which makes us wonder how it would fare on a windy day.

- *The Refrigerator Box With The Door Cut In It So You Don't Have To Climb In And Out Through The S'chach.* This is actually pretty expensive, because you have to spring for a refrigerator.

- *The Sukkah That They Have In Those Advertisements Where They Show A Guy Putting One Up In Less Than*

Four Seconds, And Another Guy Standing By With A Stopwatch And Not Helping. This breakthrough is the latest in sukkah technology, and is an excellent buy for the businessperson who is always eating on the run and is looking to set up his sukkah on an airplane wing. But good luck trying to tell the understanding and fun-loving guys at airport security why you're getting onto a plane with what appears to be a UFO strapped to your back.

Building Your Sukkah:

1. Set up all of your panels in the shape of a sukkah.

2. Walk around the sukkah whacking random parts with the hammer until everything looks pretty straight.

3. Find the box containing the rest of your sukkah parts and wonder what they're for. Dump them in the bushes.

4. Try to figure out how you're going to get the heavy furniture into the sukkah through the narrow little doorway that you made. Maybe you can drop it in through the top.

5. Get onto the stepladder and start putting up the *s'chach*. The *s'chach* is the most important part of the sukkah, so you're going to want to concentrate, rather than focus on the fact that, the more you think about it, the more you're convinced that it was a bad idea to get up on the stepladder.

6. Go inside to lie down, and let the kids put up the decorations.

Sukkah Basics

The Decorations:

One of the first things they teach you in school is that it is very important for little kids to make sukkah decorations. The basic idea is for the inside of the sukkah to look like the inside of your house. But the truth is that the only homemade art projects you have in your house are attached to your refrigerator with "Dougie's" magnets. So if you really want your sukkah to feel like home, the best idea would be to bring in your actual refrigerator, and then stick the decorations to *that*. Unless your entire sukkah is a refrigerator box.

The Lights

Most sukkahs do not come with lights, so it is up to you to find one that won't short out in the rain, or drop little pieces of electricity into your soup. Unfortunately, most of these lights are made in places like Japan, and the instructions have been translated by someone who has never really had any formal English training, but did have an extended conversation with a group of Americans once, in a dream:

For consequences that can be the finest, it is for you to knowledge that: Never to (something) these wires two times!! Or else you will be a loss of the consciousness. Also! Keep far away from fireplace, in case to be tumbled by it. If this is a maintenance achievement, kindly to place (something) in ten meters. (See drawing). Sorry to disturb.

What To Do In Your Sukkah:

You can eat in your sukkah. You can drink in your sukkah. You can even wear leather shoes in your sukkah. Once inside the sukkah, you can do whatever you would normally do in your house, only now you're doing it in a coat and mittens.

Taking Down Your Sukkah

If your sukkah is still there by the end of Yom Tov, then it is obviously very persistent, and should probably not be taken down until at least Chanukah. Plus, you're never going to be able to take out all those nails. So a good idea would be to keep the sukkah where it is, and just live in it 'til spring. That way, it'll be easier to clean your house for Pesach. Because we've all read the instruction manual on *that*, and it's a lot bigger than this one.

CONGRATULATIONS! You have just purchased your first dreidel!

No, you didn't. You've never actually purchased a dreidel in your life, have you? You wouldn't even know where to go to get a hold of one - the toy store? The plastic dreidel deposits in Central America? The candy store? Actually, that last one is not so far off if you're in the market for one of those big hollow dreidels filled with nosh. But we all know that that's not really a dreidel. That's an early *shalach manos*.

Yet you somehow have a mountain of dreidels at home, accumulated over the years from various schools, mid-winter birthday parties, early *shalach manos*, etc. But none of these dreidels came with instructions. In fact, we at the Bureau of Instruction Manuals are even led to believe that you have no idea what to do with a dreidel, which is why we came up with:

DREIDELS FOR DUMMIES:
The Instruction Manual

1. Do not swallow.

Now that we got #1 out of the way, we should also point out that THIS TOY IS NOT RECOMMENDED FOR CHILDREN UNDER THE AGE OF THREE, UNLESS THEY ARE "WITH IT" ENOUGH TO BE ABLE TO READ THIS WARNING. Small children will try to swallow anything they can get their hands on, especially dreidels, which come in colors that are similar to many of the "candies" that have been approved for use on humans. Also, small children take forever to spin the dreidel on their turn.

ORIGINS:

The dreidel originated during the times of the *Chashmona'im*, when many Jews hid away in caves to learn Torah until Greek soldiers would show up, which was when they hid their *sefarim* and pretended that they were playing an innocent game of dreidel. "Oh!" exclaimed the guards, who were somewhat relieved. "This isn't a secret yeshivah! It is simply a bunch of grown men sitting around in a cave and playing with a top!"

Nowadays, most dreidels are handed out in *cheder*, where the children practice spinning them until the *rebbi* shows up, at which time they pretend to be learning.

Dreidel for Dummies: An Instruction Manual

OBJECT OF THE GAME:

The object of the game is to win. But in case anyone asks, winning doesn't matter as long as you have fun. But there's only so much fun you can have with a game that doesn't require batteries.

MATERIALS NEEDED:

- 1 dreidel, or 1 dreidel per person, plus a pile of dreidels that everyone stays away from because they're "bad luck".

- A bunch of pennies, the exact amount depending on such factors as how many people are playing, how long the game is expected to take, and who is providing the pennies. (Beans, nuts, or Pokemon cards may also be used.)

- A hard, level playing surface, such as a dinette table, a hardwood floor, or a tennis court.

- A pan of latkes sizzling in the background. This provides atmosphere in the form of spattering noises; if the game goes into overtime, it also provides atmosphere in the form of smoke.

- 1 pot

PLAYERS:

Anywhere from 2 players to 6.4 billion players, as long as you're willing to invite complete strangers off the street to come into your home and gamble. Just keep an eye on your pennies, as well as your children.

Along with everyone else, each game of dreidel must include:

A CLEVER TITLE GOES HERE

- 1 Show-Off - This is a person, usually male, who will make sure everyone notices, at each of his turns, that he is spinning the dreidel upside down on its handle.

- 1 Dreidel-Dependent - This person will remind everyone over and over that he got the worst dreidel of the bunch and that, if anything bad happens, including the latkes exploding, it is entirely his dreidel's fault.

- 1 Floor Guy - This person cannot spin a dreidel without having it fall violently onto the floor or, if you're already playing on the floor, through the hall and down the stairs. He or she will then pick up the dreidel, announce what letter it says and throw it back into the playing area in a way that leaves the other players doubting that he's even bothered to read the dreidel. This person usually wins.

- 1 person who keeps announcing that next year he's going to bring in a weighted dreidel, so that he'll always get a "*gimmel*".

- 1 person who actually has a weighted dreidel and doesn't realize it.

GAME PLAY:

Game play begins when each player spins as many dreidels as he or she can simultaneously and then tries to choose one to use throughout the game. Allow about one hour for this.

ACTUAL GAME PLAY:

The first player spins the dreidel and waits for it to stop spinning. He then looks at it, frowns and says, "Okay, that was a practice

Dreidel for Dummies: An Instruction Manual

spin." Then he spins it again. When the dreidel finally lands on its side, the player follows the instructions corresponding to the letter shown on the dreidel:

- "NUN" - The player does nothing. He simply sits there and stares in the general direction of his dreidel until the next player gets tired of waiting and spins his own dreidel.

- "GIMMEL" - The player can do a short victory dance, and then he can take all of the pennies from the pot in the middle of the playing area. Then he can put one or two back into the pot, along with everyone else, because otherwise there's no real point in the next guy going. Or, if you want a really short game, the game is over when someone gets a "*gimmel*," and cheating is allowed.

- "HEY" - The player takes half of the pot. If there are an odd amount of pennies in the pot, a major argument ensues and the game is basically over.

- "SHIN" (also "PEY" if you have a dreidel from Eretz Yisroel, and "?" if you have one of the dreidels the *Chashmona'im* used) - The player puts some of his pennies back into the pot and then switches to another dreidel.

Game play then continues in the order in which the players are sitting, because otherwise it gets confusing.

THE WINNER:

The winner is the player who is left with the most pennies at the end of the game. He gets to keep his pennies.

THE LOSER:

The loser is the guy who supplied the pennies in the first place.

ENDGAME:

The game ends when it is time to put out the latkes. The pot could come in handy for this, but the truth is that no one really uses an actual pot. In my house, for instance, we use an ashtray.

Some people are naturally good at buying gifts. Everyone knows some hyper-organized individual – the type of person who finishes cleaning for Pesach the day after the previous Pesach, and who shows up at parties for people she doesn't even know with neatly wrapped presents that come from the heart, such as sweaters that she knitted herself in front of the fire on a couch that is covered in plastic.

But chances are that you are not that type of individual. You are an individual who, when you do remember to buy someone a present, it is usually some type of vase. But you never buy flowers, so who knows what your loved ones are using all of those vases for. Probably cereal.

And so we have compiled a short gift guide that you can read through at your leisure until you realize that we don't really know your loved ones at all, at which point you're probably just going to hand them this gift guide.

You're welcome.

NOTE: Some people may tell you that the tradition of Chanukah presents is actually copied from a similar non-Jewish tradition. This is their way of telling you that they're not getting you anything this year. In actuality, Chanukah presents came about as an offshoot of "Chanukah *gelt*", because at some point people realized that:

1. Their kids did not appreciate getting money they were not allowed to spend (with the exception of the babies, who tried to eat it), and

2. Money is what it is, whereas presents can give the illusion that you spent more than you actually did. For example, my cousin got married about six months after I did, and, while my wife and I realized that we had to get her a present, we also decided that, as a kollel couple, there was only so much we could spend on a present for a cousin to whom I had spoken maybe two words in my entire life. (I come from a big family. You can't be close with *everybody*.) So we spent about twenty minutes at Amazing Savings, and we came out with a novelty cookie jar that cost, at most, about four dollars. And then I, as the writer in the family, had to come up with a cute and funny poem comparing the sanctity of marriage to baking cookies, in the hopes that my cousin would think that I'd had this really great insight into marriage, and I had no choice but to buy her a cookie jar to illustrate it.

(As opposed to buying her a KitchenAid.) But my point is that the cookie jar was a much nicer gesture than, say, handing her a personal check for four dollars.

WOMEN: The hardest group of people to buy gifts for, speaking strictly as a man, is women. Women are highly critical of any gift that looks like a man would really like it, such as a hammock or a cordless drill. (NOTE: If you absolutely must give your wife a cordless drill, do not give it to her in person. It is far safer to mail it to her from a remote location, and then to simultaneously mail yourself somewhere even more remote.) A Woman prefers gifts that show that her husband listens to her when she's talking. For example, if your wife complains that she is overworked between cleaning the house and cooking the meals and folding the laundry and cleaning the kids and folding the meals and cooking the laundry, then you should probably get her something to show her what an attentive and caring husband you are. ("Look, honey, it's a Kitchenaid! Wait, come back! Where are you going?")

But it never hurts to get some jewelry to go along with it.

(I know this is not very original, but after five years of marriage, this is all I've gotten so far. I still don't know what I'm getting my wife. Does anyone out there want our Kitchenaid?)

MEN, OLDER BOYS, ZAIDIES, ETC.: Usually, what men get is a new work bag. Or a tie. This is despite the fact that, in almost thirty years of hanging out with men, we have never heard any of them express the slightest bit of interest in their work bag, and most of them wear the same two or three ties on an alternating basis, and keep the others in a densely-tangled clot on a tie rack in the back of the closet. What most men want is something that plugs into the wall, or doesn't have to. It doesn't even need to do anything useful.

Get a man a ratchet set, and he will happily walk around the house looking for things that need to be ratcheted. Men's gifts basically boil down to really expensive toys, although not more expensive than the toys you buy for...

BOYS: considering how easily the pieces get lost. Some of the pieces, in fact, seem to get lost in highly unlikely places, such as the washing machine, or the sewer, or deep inside your shoes. Yet somehow there are still enough pieces left to turn the floor into a minefield in the middle of the night, so that when Tatty tries to walk across the living room at four in the morning, he steps barefoot on a piece of Lego, and the entire house starts vibrating as he hops around to find a wall to lean on so that he can pull it out of his foot. So in general, you want to get your boys gifts that come in one big piece, and cannot be taken apart without access to Tatty's ratchet set. Many boys would desperately like something with wheels, such as a bike or a scooter or roller blades or one of those little red cars with the yellow tops, but they'd also be happy with a mini fridge. But we don't suggest you buy a bike, unless you want to spend the greater part of the winter repeatedly telling your son that he cannot ride in the snow. This is why *afikoman* presents were invented.

GIRLS: Most younger girls enjoy pretend play, so you can generally get them anything, from a pretend kitchen that is considerably more efficient than the one you had in your first apartment, to a pretend vacuum cleaner that used to be a real vacuum cleaner before it stopped working. A lot of little girls are also pretty happy with dolls, so that they can see what it feels like to be a real mommy, minus the carpooling and the fevers and the four A.M. feedings and the lying in bed wondering how come Tatty still hasn't come back with that baby bottle, and why the entire house is shaking.

Oy, Gevalt! I Almost Forgot!

BABIES: Babies don't really know that it's Chanukah, unless it is your very first baby, in which case you've already convinced yourself that he or she is an all-around genius, and nothing we say is going to change that. So you're going to run out and buy a baby toy, which plays the same three songs over and over and over again – but only the first four cords of these songs, because your baby keeps pressing the button to restart the songs before they finish. So maybe he isn't quite the Mensa genius you seem to think he is. In truth, though, nothing you get your baby will capture his interest as much as the wrapping paper it comes in, so we suggest you just get him a big roll of wrapping paper.

BUBBIES: Bubbies will always hand out tastefully-wrapped gifts, and then tell you that you don't have to get them anything, so the best gift for the grandmother on your list is *also* wrapping paper. It's funny how life comes full circle like that. Just make sure to wrap it in a different print so she knows when to stop unwrapping.

BOSSES: Your boss doesn't need a present, okay? Because you put in over forty hours a week, week after week, and for what? Do you even get a bonus around the holidays? Hah!

EMPLOYEES: We think you'd better give them a bonus. This is one instance where you cannot get away with a cheap gift and a nice card.

I still have not gotten myself a new menorah. Not that there's anything wrong with my old menorah, unless you count the fact that, due to extremely poor planning, the holder for my *shamash* is set directly over the fourth and fifth candles, so that the heat rises and melts it from the bottom, and as a result it keeps falling over. I do take some safety precautions, of course; I put down foil on the table, I put foil on the floor, I line the curtains with foil, etc. It's a lot like Pesach-time, but with donuts.

I don't even know how I came into possession of this menorah. I originally got it when I lived in my parents' house – at some point I got too old to use those little birthday candles, and my

"Where's my Shamash?"

mother handed me an old oil menorah she found in the back of the breakfront. No one knew where the menorah came from – we think it actually came with the breakfront. But whoever designed it was definitely spending a little too much time around oil fumes.

I don't know why it took me so long to realize what was wrong with my menorah. The first couple of years that I used it, I found myself coming back into the living room soon after I lit the candles to find that the *shamash* had buried itself in the ashtray full of dreidels that my mother leaves next to the menorahs, or that my candle had seemingly turned itself inside out, and burnt out in record time. At the time, I didn't put two and two together -- I just thought that I had the worst luck with *shamashim*, the same way that a lot of people feel that they have the worst luck with whichever dreidel they end up with, and don't stop to think that maybe the reason it keeps falling over in the same direction is because one side was melted down by a runaway *shamash*.

After a couple of years I started dorming, and set up my menorah in yeshivah alongside the other three hundred menorahs that filled the poorly ventilated basement dining area with an olive oil haze that made the guys do crazy, outlandish things, like try to light a floating wick in the yeshivah's chicken soup. (We actually did that once, and a single bowl of soup kept the wick going for over a half-hour! Not that anybody was surprised.)

Most of the boys in yeshivah did not use the same menorah that they'd used at home, because they didn't want anyone to accidentally walk off with it. I did bring the one I used at home, because I was hoping that somebody *would* walk off with it. But the rest of the guys were pretty inventive with their menorahs. Some guys had those little foil menorahs that they were amazed did not get crushed in their bags on the way back from the grocery store; some brought along the menorahs that came with *their* breakfronts; some guys turned a bunch of empty soda cans upside down and set up oil in the little groove on the bottom; and some guys had their soda cans right-side up, and filled them all of the way to the top with oil, or yeshivah chicken soup. And when my uncle was in yeshiva, he and his friends used a bunch of beer bottles. That way, if the dorm counselor would catch them drinking, they could just say, "We're making menorahs," or "We're making menorahs for next year," or "We're making menorahs to sell to raise money for the yeshivah." But no one ever bought these menorahs, so they ended up recycling them at the store for Chanukah *gelt*. Which they used to buy more menorahs.

Nevertheless, with all of the peculiar menorahs abounding, mine was the only one whose *shamash* kept falling off. This bothered me for a little while, until I realized that I could actually dispose of my *shamash* as soon as I was finished lighting, because there were actually three hundred other *shamashim* in the room.

Then at some point I got married, and mine became the only *shamash*. For now, I still dispose of my *shamash* and rely on the ten-million-watt halogen lamp that we keep right next to the menorah, but I do keep hinting to my wife that if she's ever trying to think of a good Chanukah present for her husband, and we accidentally fall into a huge load of money that the *yeshivos* have no way of knowing about, it would not be a horrible idea to buy me a really nice menorah, preferably about the size of the one outside Chabad. But my wife keeps hinting back that she doesn't really like the looks of any of the menorahs that she sees that are in our

"Where's my Shamash?"

actual price range, which includes all of the menorahs in Amazing Savings, *and* the ones at the grocery store.

But when my wife's grandfather died this past summer, I felt a renewed hope – not because he left us money, which he didn't, and not because I am an insensitive creep who feels renewed hope when people die. The man was a ninety-five-year-old widower who was legally blind, and he just wanted to be with his wife. The reason that I felt a renewed hope was that I figured I could take first crack at his menorah collection.

As a survivor of WWII who came to this country with nothing but the shirt on his back, my wife's grandfather (or "Grandpa," as most people called him) never threw out a single thing in the sixty-something years that he's been here. His house is full of busted phones from the '50s, ancient pairs of glasses, and mountains and mountains of yellow newspapers with black-and-white photos in them. (Wrap your mind around that for a second. The newspapers are yellow, but the photos are black-and-white.) On the one day that my wife and I went down to help clear out his house (before we decided that walking in there with three curious children under the age of four was pretty counterproductive), I spent a good portion of the day throwing out a huge basement pile of old flowerpots filled halfway with dirt. (I am an optimist, so I say that they were filled halfway with dirt. If I were a pessimist, I would point out that they were also half-empty.)

But our main purpose in coming down, which my mother-in-law stressed repeatedly, was to take home some paintings, as well as some menorahs. Grandpa was an avid painter in his early years, and, unlike most other painters, he was not entirely obsessed with bowls of fruit. He also kept a huge collection of assorted menorahs on the wall of his dining room, most of them unused or unusable. He had the Bird Menorah, the Set of Pipes Menorah, the Painter's Palette Menorah, the "Hey, Why Don't We Make a Menorah Out of Wood?" Menorah, a tiny menorah that was designed for actual birthday candles by someone who was not interested in his candles lasting all of the way through *Maoz Tzur*, and a large oil painting of a menorah. (Wrap you mind around *that* one.)

In the end, I did not actually find any useable oil menorahs in his collection, although if he were still alive when my wife and I magically won the lottery without ever buying a ticket, I definitely would have given him my Fire Hazard Menorah to add to his collection. In the meantime, I think I'm going to make do with what I have, and as far as a *shamash*, I'm thinking of using one of those big freestanding scented candles. I definitely could have used one of *those* in yeshivah.

I believe that it is my duty, on behalf of humor columnists everywhere, to talk about themed *mishloach manos*.

Way back when, *mishloach manos* didn't *have* themes. Mostly, they consisted of little gift bags containing a bottle of grape juice and a full pineapple. Some people also stuck in halvah, which no one ate, because no one was entirely sure what halvah *was*, and no one was brave enough to reach deep into the bag to get it, because of the pineapple. This was a wonderful system that served us well for thousands of years.

But then at some point, someone decided that *mishloach manos* had to be themed, because "Foods of Yore" was getting boring. So they decided that their *mishloach manos* would become all about the theme. For instance, some people do a color theme, wherein, for example, everything they give out on a given year is green. So they pass out green bags containing green jellybeans, pistachios, a lime, green beans, Green Giant corn, Greene's baked goods, and something moldy. Or they might do a flowerpot theme, consisting of chocolate roses, brownies (for dirt), a package of sunflower seeds, some gummy worms, and a can of pesticide. The possibilities are endless!

Although I always appreciate creativity, I rarely do themes of my own. The very first year my wife and I were married, our *sheva brachos* ended the day before Taanis Esther, and, as a result of our genius idea to spend the week traveling from Monsey to Jersey to Monsey to Baltimore to Woodmere to Monsey to Sharon, Massachusetts to Providence to Queens (and yes, that's more than seven), and then spending most of the fast day putting together our bed frames, we spent a great chunk of Purim unconscious, and the theme for the one *mishloach manos* that we managed to put together was: "Items I Brought Into the Marriage from My Dorm Room That Were Still Reasonably Sealed." We gave this to our *shadchan*. She then gave us one with a "Breakfast" theme.

Most years since then, however, my wife and I have gone with the "Items That Were on Sale the Week Before Purim" theme, which usually consists of a lot of real *chametz*. In fact, we often use Purim to get rid of a lot of the *chametz* we have around the house. Last year, in addition to our regular package, we gave someone an entire box of Snackers. But it's not like we don't get it back. One year someone gave us a pan of baked ziti and a single lollypop.

This Article Has a Theme

Talk about a random combination. This year we're giving them our leftover *cholent* and a candy necklace.

A lot of people make up a theme based on their costumes. For instance, one family we know dressed up as elephants, and gave out peanuts, peanut chews, peanut butter cups, and Bamba. This was their "Let's Kill Everyone We Know Who's Allergic to Peanuts" theme. Apparently, elephant costumes were on sale the day after Halloween, and they could only come up with the one joke. I have another friend who put on a Dr. Seuss hat, dressed his kids up as Thing One and Thing Two, and made his theme, "Green Eggs and Hamantaschen". ("I will not eat them with Yehuda, I will not eat them at the *seudah*, I will not eat them, Mr. Shmuel, I do suspect they taste like fuel.") And then there are those who decide on a theme, and then realize there really are no foods to go with that theme. Friends of ours once dressed their baby in a ladybug costume, and then gave out a ladybug theme, consisting of a small ladybug toy on wheels, a magnifying glass shaped like a ladybug, some ladybug stickers, a bottle of Coke (because it was red and black – this had to be explained to me), and some taffies (because they needed a second food). I think that when there are more toys than food in your *mishloach manos*, it's time to come up with a new theme.

Some people, in the meantime, are so desperate to have a theme that they have to include a little slip of paper with their *mishloach manos* so that their friends will realize that there's any theme at all. For instance, my aunt once received a *mishloach manos* with a Pesach theme, which included, amongst other things, a box of MUST gum, because, as the poem pointed out, "We MUST clean for Pesach." You get the feeling, reading some of these poems, that a lot of these people made up their themes based on the items they'd already planned on giving out. For instance, they may write:

"HALVAH GRAPE PURIMNAPPLE! It's the BANANAversary of the DATES that HAMANTASHEN tried to WIPES out the CHEW-CHEWish people. Lucky for us, Esther was a PLANT in the palace, and got WINDEX of the idea, and Haman got GARBAGE thrown on his HEAD OF LETTUCE! And a BOX OF SNACKERS!"

Over the years, we've seen a lot of themes come and go. Aside from the "Breakfast" theme, there is also a "Lunch" theme, which many wives give their husbands *every day of the year*, and whenever Purim comes on a Friday, half the people you know give you the "Tomchei Shabbos" theme, leaving you with enough rolls and small jars of gefilte fish that you could basically sponsor *seudah shlishis* at your shul. Most yeshivah *bachurim*, after giving the matter a lot of thought about ten minutes before *shkiyah*, give their friends the "This is What the Vending Machine Had Left" theme, and I assume that a similar thing is done at nursing homes.

If I were to do themes, I would consider going with a "Yamim Nora'im" theme, consisting of jellyfish heads, apples, honey, nearly everything in that *simanim* booklet you get in the mail, and some Kipper Snacks. I would also think about doing a "Shushan Purim" theme, consisting of a bottle of Advil, a roll of Tums, some ginger ale, Rolaids, and a bail bond.

Personally, I have nothing against themes. If the ability to express oneself creatively adds to one's enjoyment of Purim, that's great. It's a lot better than the people who give everyone pre-made *mishloach manos* from the store, which sends out the following festive Purim message: "I am too busy to throw a couple of foods

This Article Has a Theme

into a bag, so here, wrapped in over three hundred feet of noisy cellophane, is about sixteen ounces of food and the entire Sunday newspaper."

And then there are the people who make, at most, one set of *mishloach manos*, and then they just sit home all day and keep swapping. The second family that comes to the door gets the first person's package; the third person gets *his*, etc., and at the end of the day, they're left with just the last one. I don't know what they do when two people come to the door at once. I suspect that the swappers just have them trade with each other. I would, however, like to find out who these people are so that I could bury my card deep, deep in their bag, under the pineapple, so that they won't notice it, and just casually pass the package along with my card still inside. In fact, if there are enough swappers involved, I may eventually get it back.

So even though themes are unnecessary, and often painfully desperate, the main thing is that this is the way a lot of people express the joyful creativity that Purim is all about. This is also why, once they have decided on a *mishloach manos* theme, they have to make five hundred of them and send them to everyone they know, even if they are not necessarily going to be able to see these people until Shavuos. They are just eager to share their creativity. After all, not all of us have humor columns.

(We open in a cave, somewhere in the wilds of Afghanistan. A man, who is very obviously Osama Bin Laden, YS"V, is sitting at a table. Two other men are with him. The taller man is holding a video camera in front of his face, aimed at Bin Laden, and the shorter man is holding a boom mike on a stick over Osama's head. It looks like they're making a chasunah video, but they aren't. Osama already has fifty-five wives. We assume he's done with wedding videos. Osama is speaking passionately into the camera.)

OSAMA: "I think that this has gone on long enough. Last week, I bought a box of crackers. I left it on the top shelf, and now it's

A Freilichen Purim, Osama: A Purim Shpiel

gone. Now I'm not saying that anybody took it. But I did write my name in big letters on the side of the package, and it's not there anymore. We're all in this cave together; all I'm saying is a little bit of consideration wouldn't hurt. Next up, we've been getting reports of American soldiers in disguise possibly infiltrating our ranks. I want to set up patrols to look for these infidels. First patrol tonight will be Akbar, Muhammed, Abdul, Omar, and Steve. We *will* find these men. And now on to our terrorist plot: (*He unrolls a huge blueprint across the table.*) This here is my evil plan. We once attempted to board British flights and mix two liquids together on the planes. Somehow, the officials got wind of the idea, and they're not allowing any liquids to be brought on at all anymore. So here is my plan: (*He looks down to consult his notes.*) You see, little do the airlines realize that they themselves are already providing us with the very weapons we need. All we need to do is combine the vinegar in the little packets of mayonnaise with the baking soda in their toothpaste, and we can create a mini volcano in the airplane bathroom! We just need enough funding to get our men onto the planes, but we can use all of this *maaser* money we never gave out. (*He lifts a huge sack of money onto the table*) I don't know why we even *have maaser* money. But we're going to spend it. And finally, tonight, we've been getting reports of bears sleeping in the upper levels of the cave. So if possible, I would like to ask that we try to be as quiet as we can, and not shoot our guns up in the air for no reason. This has been the Inner Cave News; I'm Osama Bin Laden."

(*Osama's men back away. The boom guy lowers his mike, but the camera guy keeps it rolling. The doorbell rings.*)

BOOM GUY: "Since when do we have a doorbell?"

OSAMA: "It's probably the exterminator." (*He turns to the man with the camera.*) "Hey, Bigson, would you mind getting the door?"

BIGSON: "Yes, Father." (*He moves to answer the door.*)

BOOM GUY: "No, seriously, when did we get a doorbell?

OSAMA: "Be quiet, Littleson."

(*Bigson opens the door and gets knocked backward by four people in full bunny costumes, three of whom are wearing those big bunny heads and one of whom has it under his arm, who come running past him into the cave. They are followed by a man wearing a court jester hat and holding a boom box, which is playing the song, "LaYehudim." The bunnies, all singing "LaYehudim," grab Littleson by the arm, and start dancing in a circle, while Bigson shrugs his shoulders and starts filming them. The one bunny who's not wearing his helmet pauses for a moment, puts his helmet over Bigson's head, and then continues dancing. The court jester casually walks over to Bin Laden, who is trying to figure out what just happened.*)

JESTER: (*yelling over the noise*) "A freilichen Purim, Mr. Laden!"

(*Osama walks over and stops the music. The bunnies continue dancing silently, but Littleson pulls his way out of the circle and comes back to stand next to his father.*)

OSAMA: "Who are you? Who sent you?"

JESTER: "We're collecting for the yeshivah. The yeshivah sent us. They say you have a lot of money. You're on the list!" (*He produces a list of names from his pocket and points to it.*)

A Freilichen Purim, Osama: A Purim Shpiel

OSAMA: *(reading)* "'Laden, Osama B., 613 Cave Street.' There must be some mistake."

JESTER: "No sir. The yeshivah doesn't make mistakes. See, we're collecting so that the *bachurim* could have heat in the winter, and good food made out of actual ingredients, and..."

OSAMA: "What are you doing here?"

JESTER: "I just told you." *(He pushes the button on his CD player, and the song starts up again. The bunnies grab Osama by the arm, and yank him into the dancing circle. He struggles for a bit, and then manages to get out. The rabbits stop dancing.)*

OSAMA: "Are these guys drunk?"

JESTER: "Probably. There was a lot of booze on the plane. But I'm not drunk. I'm the designated driver. I get to show you this bracelet, and you have to give me a free Coke."

(Littleson walks over and puts a bottle of Diet Coke on the table.)

OSAMA: "What are you doing?"

LITTLESON: "He's the designated driver."

OSAMA: "They're not even supposed to be here! They're American and Jewish!"

JESTER: "Don't worry, most of us are drunk. We're not going to remember anything. Izzy here hasn't stopped drinking since nightfall..." *(He gestures toward one of the rabbits, who is attempting to drink from a large bottle of schnapps through a straw sticking out of the bottom of his helmet.)* "...and Chaim over there is wearing his entire costume backwards." *(He gestures* at Chaim, *who walks backwards into a wall.*) "And I don't know about that guy." (*He points at the third bunny.*) "He hasn't said a word since we got into the limo."

OSAMA: (*nods at the one who isn't wearing a helmet*) "And how about this one?"

THIS ONE: "The inside of my helmet smells."

OSAMA: (*motions to Bigson, who is now filming everything with the bunny helmet on his head*) "And how about that one?"

JESTER: "Not one of mine. I believe that's your son."

LITTLESON: "Do you want me to shoot them?"

OSAMA: "No shooting in the cave." (*to Bigson*) "Get that smelly thing off your head! And stop filming this!"

BIGSON: (*removing his helmet, and handing it to Izzy*) "But we film everything. How else are the infidels going to know that we mean business?"

OSAMA: "THESE ARE THE INFIDELS! THEY CAUSED 9-11!"

THIS ONE: "You caused 9-11."

OSAMA: "See? Infidels!" (*He looks over at Izzy, who has poured his schnapps into the empty helmet and is trying to drink out of it like a bowl of soup.*) "I want all of you out of this cave."

JESTER: "But what about the money? There are *bachurim* starving in America!" (*He turns the player on again, and the bunnies start dancing. Bigson instinctively picks up the camcorder and resumes taping.*)

A Freilichen Purim, Osama: A Purim Shpiel

OSAMA: (*shuts the player, but the bunnies keep dancing*) "Keep it down! You're going to wake the..." (*He looks at Bigson.*) "What are you doing?"

BIGSON: (*not putting down the camcorder*) "Sorry. Force of habit."

(*Doorbell rings again.*)

(*Two men walk in, both in Purim costumes. The first, Avrami, is a* Litvak *dressed as a chassid – fake beard, frock,* shtreimel, *etc. The second, Avremel, is a chassid dressed as a* Litvak *– his* peyos *are tied up under his felt hat, he is wearing a suit jacket over his* bekishe, *he may even be wearing an improperly-tied necktie. He is also holding a boom box and a bottle of wine. The two look at each other.*)

AVREMEL: "How did we end up in Afghanistan? I told you we should have asked for directions."

AVRAMI: "You're the one who packed the wrong CD."

AVREMEL: "I thought the label said 'Purim'! How was I to know it said, 'Kippurim'!"

AVRAMI: "It's a *chazzanus* tape. We had to listen to it all the way over here."

AVREMEL: "Whose fault was that?"

AVRAMI: "I'm going to ask for directions." (*He approaches Osama, who immediately brightens up and gives him a hug.*)

OSAMA: "Heeeeey! *Niturei*..."

AVRUMI: (*holds him at arm's length*) "Whoa, how much have you had to drink? Talk about stereotyping!"

OSAMA: "I haven't drunk anything."

AVREMEL: (*walks over to Osama and offers him wine*) "It's never too late to start! That's a great costume! Let me guess: Osama Bin Laden."

OSAMA: "I *am* Osama Bin Laden."

AVREMEL: "I got it on the first try! The real Osama is skinnier, though."

AVRAMI: "We're collecting for Tomchei Shabbos. Hit it!"

(*Avremel pushes play, and they start dancing wildly with the bunnies while the boom box plays the part of* Mussaf *that asks:* "Mi yichyeh umi yamus – *who will live, and who will die." Osama stops the tape.*)

OSAMA: "This is *my* cave!"

AVREMEL: (*stops dancing and begins to light a cigarette*) "But it's Purim!"

OSAMA: "No smoking in the cave."

(*Izzy hands the empty bunny head to Avremel, who sighs and throws in his cigarette. Bunny #3, who we haven't heard from yet, takes off his helmet, and we see that he has half-a-dozen cigarettes in his mouth, his face is red, and his helmet is full of smoke.*)

BUNNY #3: (*cough, cough*) "But it's Purim!" (*cough, cough*)

OSAMA: "No smoking." (*points to a sign that says,* "Thank you for not smoking.")

AVRUMI: "Come on, have a drink! You're so tense!"

A Freilichen Purim, Osama: A Purim Shpiel

OSAMA: "I'm not going to have a drink! I want everybody out of my cave!"

BIGSON: "Not so loud, you're going to wake the…"

(*He stops talking when he notices a little boy, not much older than three, and dressed in a full Osama costume, walking in holding a nicely wrapped* **mishloach manos.** *Everyone watches as he marches right up to Osama and hands him the package. Osama has no idea what to make of this.*)

LITTLE OSAMA: "A Freilichen Purim!"

BIGSON: "Wait." (*He pulls out a second bottle of Coke and an open box of crackers with the name "OSAMA" clearly written on the side, and hands them to the child, who runs out of the cave.*)

BIG OSAMA: "What was that?" (*He stares at the package.*) "Ooh, there's halvah!"

LITTLESON: (*looking over his shoulder*) "And what are those?"

JESTER: "Those are Hamantaschen." (*He taps Osama's turban.*) "Someday we're going to make cookies shaped like this thing, too."

OSAMA: "Haman?"

AVRAMI: "Yeah, Haman was the one who adopted Esther and saved the Jewish people."

AVREMEL: "That was Mordechai."

IZZY: (*Takes off his own helmet, and takes another swig from the public-use helmet.*) "No, that was Haman."

(*At that point, an argument breaks out as to which was Haman, and which was Mordechai, with Bigson somehow also taking part in the argument. Chaim, the backwards bunny, walks over to the table to join in, and knocks over the open Diet Coke, spilling it all over Osama's blueprints.*)

OSAMA: "My evil plan!" (*He whips the towel off of his head and begins frantically cleaning up the mess.*) "Alright, that's it! Everyone out of my cave! No one is getting this money. No one!"

(*An Arab walks in, towel on his head and all. Osama hands him the money.*)

OSAMA: "You! Take this money and go! Now none of you will get it!"

ARAB: "Wow! Thank you so much! *Tizku l'mitzvos!*" (*He turns to the all of the people in costumes.*) "All right, guys, let's go!"

(*They all walk out of the cave in a single file, including Bigson, who is still taping everything.*)

JESTER: "Where are we going next?"

ARAB: "Iran."

OSAMA: "WAIT! Oh, it's hopeless." (*He turns around to see someone in a bear costume come out of the inner cave.*) "Go on, get out. All of the other Jews left already."

(*The lights go out. We hear a growl.*)

OSAMA: "Oh."

Asking For Trouble

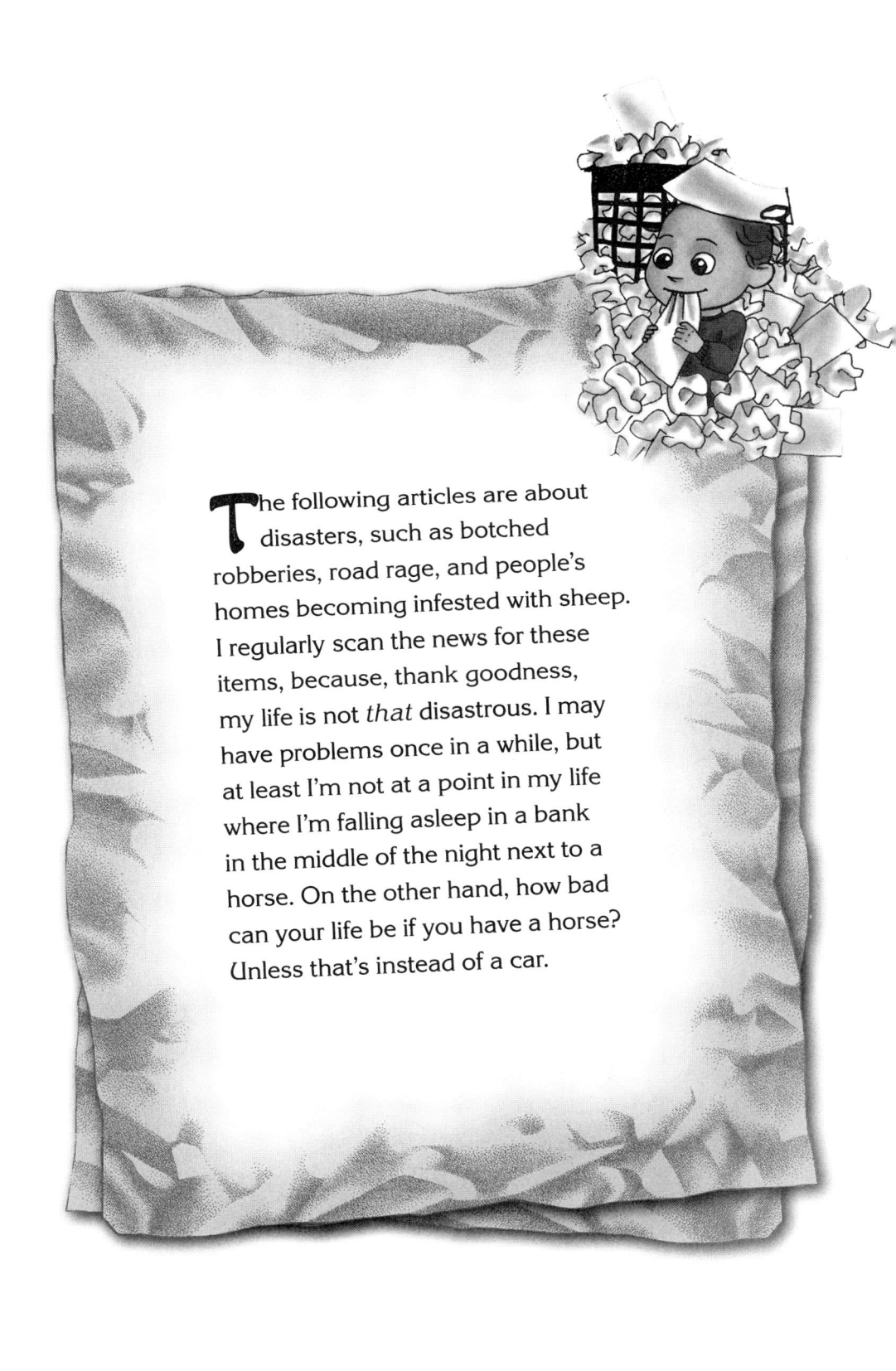

The following articles are about disasters, such as botched robberies, road rage, and people's homes becoming infested with sheep. I regularly scan the news for these items, because, thank goodness, my life is not *that* disastrous. I may have problems once in a while, but at least I'm not at a point in my life where I'm falling asleep in a bank in the middle of the night next to a horse. On the other hand, how bad can your life be if you have a horse? Unless that's instead of a car.

Numbers, People!

Let me start off by saying that I've never been part of Hatzolah. I deeply admire what they do, and it's not that I'm not inspired, but I have what the medical community refers to as "trouble getting out of bed". If I were a member of Hatzolah, and a call came in at three in the morning, the other members of my team would have to swing by my house on the way to the call to help pull me out of bed, and then they'd have to pause again once they got to the patient's house in order to roll me off the stretcher.

Nevertheless, I *am* close with a lot of the people who are actually involved in Hatzolah. In fact, Hatzolah makes up about sixteen percent of my shul, until such time as a call comes in, at which point they are out of there so fast that their *talleisim* are still hovering in place for a couple of seconds before settling on their chairs, as if these guys just vanished into thin air. And from what I hear, if there's one thing that really bugs the good men of Hatzolah, aside from getting called away in the middle of making an omelet so that they can come look at a rash or chauffeur someone to a doctor's appointment, it's that people are just not taking care of their house numbers.

You know how it can be. How often have you found yourself looking for a particular house, driving around town at dusk at roughly one mile per hour, squinting around for any numerical sign to assure you that you're even on the right block?

"You can't miss it," they told you over the phone. "It's next to the one with the fountain."

"What's the house number?" you asked.

"There's a fountain," they said. "It's right next door. And my black Camaro is in the driveway."

Or else they give you some other clue. "It's the eighth house from the end," they say.

"So you want me to drive to the end, turn around, and count eight houses?" you ask.

"No, silly," they tell you. "It's a one-way street!"

But is *your* house any better? Has anybody ever mentioned to you that they had some trouble finding your house, only you glossed over it because you weren't exactly looking for an actual answer when you asked them how the drive was? Do you excuse this by saying, "Anyone who knows me knows where I live"? What

Numbers, People!

about Hatzolah? Do *they* know where you live? Is sixteen percent of *your* shul in Hatzolah, too?

When you have a *simchah*, you put out balloons so that the *mechutanim* can find your house. Do you also put out balloons when you're having a heart attack?

"But I don't plan to *have* a heart attack," you might be saying to yourself. "I take good care of my body. I gave up fried foods, and trans fats, and soda, and carbs, and sautéed foods, and anything else that tastes halfway decent, and I have a treadmill buried under that big pile of clothes somewhere, and no one ever jumps out of closets and yells, 'Boo!' at me and almost gives me a heart attack. And I never get into accidents either, because I don't leave roller skates on the stairs, and I keep my pot handles pointed at the inside of my cabinets, and I wear a seat belt and a bike helmet, often at the same time. Plus, I'm going to live forever."

To that we say: We hope you're right (although we don't want to eat at your house on Shabbos). But if anyone else on your block requires the services of Hatzolah, from, say, trying to avoid you on the street and running into a mailbox, then don't you think that Hatzolah will find this guy faster if everyone on your block had a visible house number? Probably not, because he's lying right there in the middle of the sidewalk. But you see our point.

And then there are the people who think they have adequate house numbers, and can't imagine why they have to peer out their windows every other morning to see their carpool beeping in front of someone else's house. If you are one of these people, you have to ask yourself: Are my numbers big enough? Are they blocked from certain angles by tree branches, or shadows, or tall grass, or that big honking SUV that has been squatting in front of your house ever since you moved in? Do you have black numbers on a navy blue house? Do you have numbers on your front door, so that they disappear when you open it? Do you have numbers on your *back* door, because that's the one you always use? Do you have your numbers on your garbage can, and if so, are you always aware of when they're rolling down the block?

And what kind of print do you have? Do you have the kind where the number one looks like a seven, and the six looks like an eight, and the two looks like a script "Q"? And speaking of script, are your numbers written in script? Why? Do you think it makes you look educated, so that people will say, "Wow, he actually finished third grade"? Hatzolah is supposed to be able to read your numbers in their sleep, but it takes actual brainpower to read words. Imagine if your alarm clock said "SIX THIRTY-TWO" in script. You would *never* get out of bed. In fact, just look at the Ancient Romans. They all thought it was a great idea to put up Roman Numerals on their houses, until the time came when EMS found themselves zooming around town on their little rickshaws, trying to remember which number "L" stood for. This could be why we tend to see so few Romans around today.

Here's a good way to tell if you need to do something about your house numbers. Stand on the sidewalk in front of your house and make sure that you can see your numbers. Can you see them? Good. Now back up a couple of steps until you're almost in the street and try again. Can you still see them? Keep backing up until you're standing smack dab in the middle of the street. Do you see all of the cars swerving to avoid hitting you? At this rate, you should *definitely* do something about your house numbers.

Numbers, People!

Of course, after all this, there are still people who are not going to do anything about it. They're going to read this article, laugh at the jokes, and then go back to being oblivious to the fact that this article was directed at *them*. So what should Hatzolah do about these people? Sure, they can impose thousand-dollar fines, like the police do in certain parts of Maryland, and then use the proceeds to pay for some of their major expenses, such as fueling the trucks. But what if people don't want to pay? Hatzolah is not just going to refuse care; they're Hatzolah – they'd never do that.

Our suggestion, of course, is that Hatzolah do the exact opposite – they should GIVE these people care. If someone refuses to pay the fine, Hatzolah should smash into his house in the middle of the night and load him onto a stretcher, and then bring him to the hospital, and say the following words, which are not entirely untrue: "There is something wrong with this person, and we are not sure what it is." Then they can stand back and watch the doctors perform exploratory tests until his insides look like mayonnaise.

But then, that is just our suggestion. And that's why we're not in Hatzolah.

This article's important topic is: Traffic Safety. Most people don't really take the time to stop and think about traffic safety, unless they are in front of me at busy intersections. Then they can stop and think for hours. Sometimes days. But I don't get mad, because I know that this is what they are doing, and they can't very well think about traffic safety while they're are doing seventy-miles-per-hour on the highway. That time is for making phone calls. But I do know that, while I am behind them, right in the middle of the intersection with the light about to change, the only thought going through *my* mind is *definitely* traffic safety.

But at least we *have* traffic lights, as opposed to some of the cities in Europe.

Caution: No Signs Ahead

I am referring here to an article sent in by alert reader Rachel Weiner of Brooklyn, NY, concerning a growing number of cities in Europe that have done away with all of their traffic signs. This includes red lights, Stop signs, Yield signs, One Way, No Parking, Merge, Slippery When Wet, Stop Sign Ahead, Goat Crossing, Slow Children, Bump, Dip, and Bridge Out. In addition, they have done away with the lines in the middle of the roads, raised the street so it is level with the sidewalks, and covered the whole thing in cobblestones. So if Europe collapses within the next few years, we'll know why.

This move, which was dubbed the "Shared Space Project" because of the way drivers, cyclists, and pedestrians are forced to use the same unmarked public surface, is the brainchild of Dutch Traffic Engineer Hans Monderman. But before you start wondering if maybe Hans got hit by a few too many pedestrians, I should point out that, for the most part, his experiments have been a success. The Dutch Town of Makkinga, for example, has been without road signs since 1991, although, granted, it has a population of one thousand people. (The article does not say what the population was before they removed the road signs). No offense to the Dutch, but even if half of the town decides to show flagrant disregard for the other drivers, it will still be nothing compared to ten-thousand minivans trying to do carpool outside the *yeshivah ketanah* and competing for that one little parking spot in front of the doors.

But the Shared Space Project has taken effect in other cities, too. The city of Drachten in the Netherlands has removed their signs seven years ago, and there have been absolutely no traffic fatalities since, but that could be because no one is exactly sure where the Netherlands are to begin with. Even the Netherpeople don't know for sure. But Hans somehow found his way out of there, and is bringing his project to cities in England, Belgium, and Germany, which, according to the article, has six hundred forty-eight different traffic signs, not that anyone is surprised. I think that a lot of people would pay good money to watch the Shared Space Project come to Germany.

Monderman proclaims that streets today should be like they were in the Middle Ages, when horse carriages, pedestrians, handcarts, and often cattle scurried about the cobblestone streets in a totally unregulated fashion, and you never read in the history books about people getting into traffic accidents. (Maybe he thinks there was something in the cobblestones.) Never mind that the worst thing that could have happened back then was two donkeys crashing into each other at five miles per hour or taking a nap in the crosswalk. He says that streets today could be like ice-skating rinks, where there are absolutely no markers, but people merge in and go pretty much in the correct direction and usually at about the same speed as everyone else.

I have to admit, reading this does make me a little nervous. I don't know about you, but when I go to an ice-skating rink, which I do about every third Chanukah, I am not exactly a model of Shared Space. I spend a lot of time moving along the wall, and when I don't, I skate around as quickly as I possibly can, hoping that my momentum will keep me aloft, similar to how airplanes work. And then at some point I head back for the wall, but I don't want to slow down as I approach it or else I'll fall, so WHAM! I believe this is why professional hockey players are missing so many teeth. But occasionally I do fall, and at that point my prime focus becomes rolling – like a kid rolling down a hill – at top speed

Caution: No Signs Ahead

toward whichever wall is closest, because I am terrified off the blades, as well as the thought that the people behind me are as bad at stopping as I am.

But ice-skating rinks notwithstanding, the plan has a sound philosophical backing. The basic idea is that people are bad drivers because there are so many traffic regulations. For example, a lot of people (except for the guy who drives in front of me every single time I'm out on the road) speed through yellow lights in hopes that that they won't get stuck at red ones.

Proponents of the plan also point out that having so many signs about is dumbing down the average driver, who will figure that, if there is no "Slippery When Wet" sign on a road, that road is made out of a special kind of tar that is actually NOT slippery when wet. Seriously. And "BEWARE OF PEDESTRIANS"? Is there anyone who sees a pedestrian on the road and does not know to beware?

This, says Hans, is the reason for his program. The benefit of Shared Space, he says, is that there are no rigid rules, and you're never sure exactly what's going to happen, so you drive around slowly and cautiously and leave actual finger indentations on the steering wheel. Also, coffee sales go up. It all has to do with something called "Risk Compensation". Risk compensation means that people will not go bungee jumping unless you tie a cord around their ankles. If there's no cord, chances are they're going to look for a safer way off the bridge.

A side benefit of the plan, Hans says, is that it forces drivers to be more courteous to one another. He envisions a day when the program will spread all over the world. I could just see it coming to New York City.

FIRST CAB DRIVER (gesturing toward the intersection): "After you."

SECOND CAB DRIVER (gesturing back): "No. After *you.*"

FIRST CAB DRIVER: "After *you.* I insist."

SECOND CAB DRIVER: "No, after you. You're a guest in this country."

But many people are still skeptical. They say that the whole thing sounds like anarchy, and that the person with the biggest vehicle is always going to have the right of way. (This could be a huge problem in America, where our vehicles often grow bigger overnight.) They're not either thrilled with the prospect of people who actually *aren't* bright enough to be able to think on their own, or with visions of people having to cross busy streets in groups.

Personally, I don't think the plan will ever get that far, because I think that, as a nation, Americans have proven that we are not exactly the brightest headlights on the road. I just mention all of this to let you know that, on your next trip to Europe, it would probably be a good idea to take a lot of side roads and shortcuts through people's houses. Or you can just go to Venice, because what's the worst thing they can do *there*?

(PLEASE NOTE: The following stories are not made up. In truth, none of the things I write about are made up – part of the point of my column is to laugh about the craziness going on around us instead of panicking about it. But this time, you're going to read the article and say to yourself, "There is no way he didn't make this up." This is because the very fact that you can read at all shows that you are way more intelligent that most of the people in these stories. Your only problem is that you say things to yourself.)

I've been thinking a lot about this recent crime wave we've been having. Take, for example, the AP article about a man who was apprehended on charges of robbery, handcuffed, and loaded into the back of a squad car. The man waited patiently until the car was stopped at a red light, at which point he kicked out the window and dove headfirst through the hole into the snow.

Unfortunately for him, that was about as far as he'd thought things through. Staggering to his feet, he ducked into the nearest building, barreled down the hallway, and hid behind a door. Strategically, this was probably not his best option. Considering that the cops knew exactly which building he'd run into, it would only be a matter of time before they found him HIDING BEHIND A DOOR. But for all we know, he had a plan. Either way, he probably should have read the big sign above the door to the building, because the building he'd ducked into was actually the county sheriff's office. This reminds me of the story a couple of months back where a guy tried to hold up a Wal-Mart, and did not realize that there was some kind of police convention going on there, because he failed to notice the SEVENTY-FIVE POLICE CARS SITTING IN THE PARKING LOT.

But getting back to our genius behind the door, an elderly deputy noticed him running down the hall, and the fact that he was handcuffed and covered in snow raised some red flags. So the deputy just walked over and held onto him until the cops ran in. We're guessing they were trying to find a parking space.

Our second story involves two men in North Carolina who actually broke into a police station to steal "flagpoles, flags, and a sign". When police later investigated the door that had been damaged during the break-in, they found that it was smeared with birthday cake and frosting.

According to reports, the suspects were seen earlier that evening eating cake at a birthday party in a restaurant. We don't know what

When Facing Muggers, Always Carry a Handkerchief

was in the cake, but it must have been pretty good, because they went straight from there to stealing flagpoles at the police station. When the men were caught later that evening, says Police Detective Aimee Sumner, with a straight face, "They had cake and icing all over them."

How old are these guys? Two?

Sumner says that officers had no trouble finding the suspects, because as soon as they were able to tear the police dogs away from the door, they actually found a crumb trail leading out to the main street. Picture it: these two guys are coming out of a birthday party, and they are just covered in frosting, to the point that everything they touch gets frosted. Not only that, but they are so caked in the stuff that it is just plopping off of them in chunks as they run down the street. The two guys look each other up and down, and decide that the best possible course of action is to play "Capture the Flag".

If that is not enough to convince you that we are in the middle of a crime wave, consider our next story involving a twenty-two-year-old Alabama man named Daniel, who was charged with stealing $300 from his grandfather. It all started at about 1:30 on a Tuesday afternoon, when Daniel was feeling a bit low on cash, which is understandable, seeing as he was home at 1:30 on a Tuesday afternoon. So he decided that the best way to get more was to rob someone, but he wasn't feeling up to the whole process of finding a victim and driving all of the way over to their house, so instead he put on a ski mask, grabbed a tire iron, and walked a whole ten feet to his grandfather's house next door.

When Daniel entered the house, he found that his grandfather was taking his afternoon siesta. So he marched right into the bedroom, brandished his tire iron, and said, "This is a robbery. I need your money, and I mean it, Pa-Paw."

It was at this point that Daniel realized that his grandfather did not actually have his money on him—his wallet was in his pants, hanging over a chair. So Daniel grabbed the pants and ran out of the room, through the kitchen, toward the back door.

Now, at this point, his grandfather had had it. With most muggings, the most they get away with is your wallet, and maybe your watch or jewelry. But it is very rare for them to make off with your actual pants. So the grandfather did what any good grandfather would do, given the circumstances. He tackled him. If there's anything worse than having your pants stolen by your grandson in the middle of your afternoon nap, it's having your seventy-year-old grandfather tackle you in his pajamas in the kitchen.

After a brief scuffle, Daniel fled back to his house, leaving behind —you guessed it—a trail of cake crumbs. Okay, it wasn't cake crumbs, but what he actually dropped, in the ten-foot run back to his house, was the pants, the billfold, a five-dollar bill, and the tire iron. So the police arrested him. Daniel, of course, denied that he was the man under the ski mask. Apparently, it was someone else who had access to his grandfather's bedroom and called him "Pa-Paw".

But that is not all. I was going to post another story, although I am out of space, about a homeowner in Westchester who was awakened in the middle of the night by someone breaking in through his kitchen door, which is probably the craziest door to break into, because for all one knows, the homeowner can be standing on the other side of the door with any one of hundreds of kitchen implements. I am reminded of a story wherein someone tried to break into my friend's house through the kitchen door on a Friday night, and came face to face with my friend's uncle, who was holding a challah knife, and the intruder basically tripped over himself trying to get back out the door. In this case, however, the homeowner, fearing for the safety of his wife and children, sprayed the intruder in the face with a fire extinguisher, and then hit him with it, thus demonstrating the importance of always keeping a fire extinguisher in your kitchen in case of emergencies.

So this is where we stand. Frankly, if this is what passes for a crime wave these days, I am relieved. I just bring these stories to your attention to let you know that if you ever come face to face with a criminal, don't panic, because chances are he's more scared than you are. The best thing to do is just keep your head, look him in the eye, and wipe the frosting off his face. After all, he has to look good for his mug shots.

Mooving Around

This article's topic is "Barnyard Animals in Strange Places". And for good reason:

Our first story concerns a man in Germany (frequent readers of my column will notice that an alarming percentage of these stories happen in Germany), named Stephan Hanelt, who arrived at the bank early one morning to use the ATM, and found himself face to face with a horse. The horse was just standing around in the bank vestibule, minding its own business; at least as much as a horse could, given the circumstances.

Now, I know what you're thinking. You're thinking that the horse probably belonged to a police officer. I live near New York City, and

Moving Around

I occasionally see a mounted police officer, way up on his horse, afraid to get down, looking out on everyone and everything with the vigilant eye of a man who is wondering how on earth he's ever going to get a bad guy back to the police station if he does get to chase one down. These policemen go everywhere on their horses – crime scenes, demonstrations, Dunkin Donuts, etc. So it's not so hard to imagine an officer going to the bank on his horse, and then maybe getting knocked off by a short doorway so that he ended up locked outside the bank with his horse stranded inside with all of the officer's bank cards and identification and driver's licenses and so on. But that is not how the horse got there. In fact, if Stephan would have stayed for a moment longer before he bolted out of the bank, he might have noticed a man sleeping near the horse's feet.

In actuality, the horse belonged to a man named Wolfgang Heinrich, who was attempting to ride home from the bar the night before, but, as he was too drunk to be riding a horse, he kept nodding off and then awakening with a start, which is a very scary thing to do when you're sitting on a horse. And as he kept nodding off, the following questions kept popping back into his head:

1. Since when do I have a horse?
2. Where did I park it while I was at work? and
3. How do I get home from here?

Wolfgang decided that he was too tired to ride home. So he found a nearby bank, and used his bank card to let himself in, kind of like at a hotel, except that most hotels frown on horses, even in the parking lot. Maybe he wanted to see if he could put it in a safe deposit box for the night.

So Stephan, who did not want to go ahead and punch in his ATM code with a horse looking over his shoulder, ran off and came back with a cop, who let Wolfgang off with a warning. At some point, someone with a camera phone had the foresight to take a picture, which I have had the pleasure of seeing, and in which the horse is standing over his master, who is still sleeping, and the horse has an expression on its face that says, "Oh, great. Not again!"

Our second story involves a woman in Wyoming by the name of Shirley Weidt, who, despite both the AP *and* newspaper running stories about her, really wishes people would stop making a big deal about the goat she has living in her minivan. After all, she says, she has taken the seats out, and is keeping the goat fed and watered, and it's not like she's baking *matzos* back there. In fact, the city animal control officer agrees that she isn't treating the goat cruelly or violating any rules or anything, but that she will have to get the goat out of there before it starts getting hot outside. But it does make you wonder, when you buy a pre-owned minivan, exactly what the previous owners did with it.

But her neighbors are concerned, and they're not sure why. Being concerned is just something that neighbors do. They would prefer that she keeps the goat in a shed, even though the average shed does not have nearly as much fast food scattered around on the floor. It's all the fault of the sales staff at the car dealership, really. Shirley asked them point-blank how many kids she could get into the van, and they just assumed that she meant children. But in Wyoming, you have to ask.

But neighbors will always make a big deal. In December, police in North Carolina responded to a call about a man who was keeping eighty sheep in his house, probably for insulation. Needless to say, the man lived alone – besides for the eighty sheep, of course. He was the only human there, though. And it is entirely possible that

Mooving Around

he had no idea how many sheep he had, and that whenever he tried counting them he fell asleep. Sometimes people start doing something with good intentions, and then they find themselves in over their heads.

But what phone number does a neighbor even call to report something like this? Isn't 911 for emergencies only?

"Officer, please hurry! This man has eighty sheep in his house!"

"All of a sudden? What did he do?"

"No, it's been like this for a while. But they keep eating my newspapers!"

Honestly, I don't know how a guy could live with eighty sheep in his house. How does he get anything to eat? I remember the last time I was at a petting zoo – it was an overcast day, and my wife and I were the only ones there. I decided to splurge on one of those waffle cones full of that animal food that looks like Fiber One, but as soon as the attendant handed me the cone, the animals were all over me. I was surrounded, and with every passing second all of the animals inched forward, and I knew that, although they were not supposed to bite, I had no guarantee that none of them, in their eagerness to beat the other animals to the Fiber One, would nick my finger by accident. (I've been in yeshivah; I know how it works.) So I found myself trying to placate them with one piece at a time, shrieking like a little girl every time one of them lunged for a piece in my hand, and consistently inching backward, until I eventually found myself scattering pieces randomly and running backward, with the entire population of the petting zoo racing after me. By the time I got back to my wife, I had nothing left – not even the cone, which was just as well, because after seeing what had happened to me, my wife was no longer interested in feeding the animals. So I don't see how this guy gets anything to eat *ever*, with eighty sheep running into the kitchen every time he opens the fridge.

Our final story concerns an AP article about police in Kaliningrad, Russia, who caught a man driving a stolen passenger bus, and when they pulled it over, lo and behold, they found five head of cattle on it. It turns out, the man was a cattle wrangler who, along with an accomplice, had stolen some cows and were trying to sneak them out of town so that they wouldn't just wander back home in the middle of the night. But how do you sneak five cows out of town unnoticed? So they stole a bus. The two had also stolen a car, but that was wishful thinking.

So we have to say that the situation is very serious. Where are barnyard animals going to turn up next? The supermarket? The DMV? Running for office? I say we should -- Hey, who let all these sheep into my house? Get away from me! What are you doing – get off the keyboaklndbnfgblknfgblf

I know this is no way to start off a humor column, but summer safety is no laughing matter. Children in particular are known to be very good at finding new and inventive ways to hurt themselves. If you are responsible for any children, or have someone sitting next to you who is responsible for some children but is for some reason weeping into her hands, you need to make sure that you are always aware of the basic rules of safety. This safety quiz will test your knowledge:

1. As a parent, which of these dangers are you most worried about when it comes to your children?

    a. Strangers with candy.

A CLEVER TITLE GOES HERE

  b. Strangers with non-kosher candy.
  c. Metal slides on hot days.
  d. Babies eating grass.
  e. Paper cuts reading this book.

2. **Complete the following statement. "Bike helmets...**
  a. Should be worn whenever you ride a bike, and possibly even when you're working on the roof of your garage."
  b. Make you look like a giant mushroom."
  c. Should really be made to cover the entire head, like a motorcycle helmet, except that if they did, parents would not be able to recognize their children when it's time for dinner."
  d. Are a good alternative to yarmulkes, because of the chin straps."

3. **Before your kids leave the house, you make sure they are wearing...**
  a. A layer of suntan lotion deep enough to conceal a set of keys.
  b. Bright colors, because dark colors absorb sunlight (with the exception, somehow, of sunglasses).
  c. Dark colors, because bright colors attract bugs.
  d. Stripes, like a zebra. Let's see what happens.

4. **If your children are going to be riding their bikes on the street, what steps do you take to make sure they are safe?**
  a. You make sure that they know the proper hand signals, despite the fact that most of the drivers out there have no idea what they mean. No one can

No Laughing Matter

remember which signal means, "I'm about to make a right turn," and which one means, "I'm about to stop," and which one means, "I am about to say, 'Hello'."

b. Let them do what they want, so long as they don't talk on their cell phones while they are riding.

c. Get them a set of blinkers, bearing in mind that since they're driving skinny little bikes, a lot of the motorists are going to have trouble figuring out whether the flashing light is their left blinker or their right one.

d. I get out there in my vest and direct traffic.

5. When driving around town during the summer, you…

a. Count your kids every time you get into or out of the car.

b. Put on oven mitts before touching the steering wheel.

c. Avoid leather seats.

d. Brush up on your hand signals.

6. How do you keep your kids from running into the street?

a. Give them a long speech featuring lots of color slides, and occasionally let them read horror stories in the newspaper. Sure, getting them to fall asleep later that night is going to be an issue, but that is not our problem. We're just a safety article.

b. Don't coat them in sun block. Kids are slippery enough as it is.

c. Keep them in the house until they are bouncing off the walls and having water fights with that hose that pulls out of your kitchen sink.
d. Move to a meadow.

7. Poison ivy has...
    a. Three leaves.
    b. Four leaves.
    c. Six hundred thirteen leaves.
    d. I don't know. I live in Brooklyn.

8. What precautions do you take before going on family trips?
    a. I make sure each of my kids can recite his name, address, and telephone number, and if my child has a name that is hard for the general public to pronounce, I make sure he knows how to spell it.
    b. I stock up on barbecue corn chips.
    c. I put distinctive matching outfits on all of my children, as well as on my husband.
    d. I leave the kids at home with my in-laws. That way I know where both of them are.

9. The best answer to all of these questions is:
    a. A.
    b. C.
    c. B.
    d. None of the above.
    e. All of the above, except D.

10. While you've been working on this quiz, your child:
    a. Ate something with three leaves.
    b. Drank all of the sun block.

No Laughing Matter

      c. Schlepped his bike up to the top of a slide.
      d. Moved to a meadow.

It's not easy, keeping your kids safe. The clothes that drive away the sun attract bees. Sun block makes your kids slippery. And hand signals seem useless when no one you are signaling knows what you're trying to tell them. But if there is one thing that you can take logical steps to avoid, it is heat exhaustion.

Everyone has their safety topic that they are especially paranoid about, and mine is heat exhaustion. (At least for now.) I am the guy who always runs into the middle of the dancing circle at a wedding with a glass of water for the *chassan*, usually spilling some of it on at least six people, although it's not a big deal, because it's just water. Except for when it's Coke. And there's no way the caterer will ever see that particular glass again.

Children, in particular, are more susceptible to heat exhaustion, because they are smaller. Think of how long it takes to bake cookies, as opposed to how long it takes to bake a cake. Plus, kids don't always notice when they're dehydrating, just like kids never notice when they're tired. They just think that, after a certain time of night, the world gets funnier, then it gets meaner, and then it gets chillier.

The best way to combat heat exhaustion, of course, is to keep drinking. You can drink while you're working, or learning, or playing, or walking, or leaning left. You can even drink and drive, for all I care. But bear in mind that alcohol makes you sweat more, so you should definitely stick to water. Especially if you're going to be outside. For instance, if you're planning on spending an entire day in an amusement park, make sure that at least one person in your party is lugging around what is essentially an entire knapsack filled with water (along with maybe some double-wrapped sandwiches floating around in it, but that is a topic for another day).

But a lack of drinking is not the only way a child can suffer from heat exhaustion. There was a story in the news about a woman in New Hampshire by the name of Sandi Fontaine who baked cookies on the dashboard of her car. (I guess she figured, she already has her oven mitts in there, she may as well bake cookies.) She left the car outside her place of work in the morning with two pans of raw cookie dough, and within a couple of hours she was able to treat her coworkers to fresh cookies. "My husband wanted me to run some errands this morning," she told reporters. "But I said, 'I can't. I'm baking cookies.'"

Do you know how, when you open the car door on a hot day, the heat comes out and punches you in the face? When Sandi opened her door, she was hit with the smell of fresh cookies.

I don't know how I can be any more blatant as to what I'm saying. After all, this is a humor column.

It's All the Rage

There is no area in which we need more work than the area of anger, at least for the purposes of this article. But anger is not always a bad thing. In fact, we are taught that in certain situations, it is good to get angry. Of course, it's very hard to judge what those situations are, so the best thing to do is to call your rabbi. Do you notice how your rabbi is not angry, even though you called him at two in the morning? That is what *you* have to strive for.

The key to dealing with anger is to figure out exactly what it is that makes us mad. Experts agree that one of the leading causes of anger in our society is marriage. Get two people under the same roof, and no matter how much they like each other, they're occasionally going to get into loud shouting matches over issues such as thermostat settings. This seems strange, because you have friends that you barely even like, but in all the years you have never once raised your voice to them, even that time when they whipped their *tallis* around and got you in the eye. Yet you will scream and shout at your spouse if she so much as... What did she do again? You have no idea. But that is not the point.

What is it that makes you fight so much with the one person who supposedly means more to you than anyone in the world? Maybe it's the thought that, whatever it is they did, such as that they left dirty socks on the coffee table, it is magnified by the idea that you're going to have to keep correcting this behavior for the rest of your life. You have done the math, and it turns out that if your husband leaves every other pair of socks on the table for the next ninety years, you will altogether have picked up over twelve thousand pairs of socks. And that scares you. You may need a bigger coffee table.

So the two of you launch into a whole argument that often lasts days, and that each of you absolutely *has* to win, with bonus points awarded based on how many doors you slam. The two of you will march around the house going in and out of rooms for the sole purpose of slamming doors, until your husband somehow manages to strand himself on the front porch with his socks still off. So this is definitely a problem.

Another leading cause of anger is computers. Every once in a while your computer gets into a big snit wherein it refuses to do anything, and instead shows you an hourglass symbol, which pretends to pour sand back and forth for a good half hour despite the fact that there is no actual sand in your computer, and all you

It's All the Rage

want to do is shake the monitor and shout, "Where is the sand going now, huh?" But that would just be shooting the messenger. The real culprit is the computer itself, which is hiding down under your desk and making whirring noises like it's actually thinking. And so you turn it off, because sometimes that helps it forget whatever it was that was bothering it and come back on like nothing happened. Only now it says that you've shut it down improperly. The *toaster* never complains when you shut it down improperly. And now the computer says that it has to check if any data was lost, and you want to shout, "Where could it have gone? Into the WALL?" And then you call customer support so that someone could put you on hold and go to lunch. At ten in the morning.

Another major cause of rage is bad drivers. Sometimes you're sitting in your car waiting to get off the highway at, say, Exit 1, and there is actually a long line of cars waiting to get off, and you have places to go and your air conditioner doesn't work and you get the feeling that you're moving backwards because you just saw a sign for Exit 2, when all of a sudden some driver comes along and zooms to the head of the line, like why should he have to wait with all of the *regular* people? And why are they honking at him? Can't they see he's on the phone?

And then you get onto another road, and there is someone in front of you in the "passing" lane, despite the fact that he is not passing anybody, and has never passed anybody in his entire life, and his left blinker is on. And then you end up at a traffic light behind a driver who is stunned – *stunned* – when the light turns green, as if that's the *last* thing he expected it to do, so now he has to sit there for about 30 seconds absorbing the stunningness of it all and trying to figure out what on Earth he should do now. And you find yourself sitting there wishing you had a giant paintball cannon mounted on the roof of your car so that you can push a button and SPLAT! His car would be engulfed in a wad of paint. *Green* paint. Wouldn't that be GREAT?

I mean terrible. "Wouldn't that be terrible?" is what I meant. But we see that we can definitely get carried away when we're upset, which is why it is very important to have a way to deal with it.

One idea, experts suggest, is to think over what you're about to do, and whether it will cause a chain of events that you will end up regretting. There was a story in the news about a man in Germany who got into a nasty argument with his wife, and decided, in a fit of rage, to cut his entire single-story house in half with a chainsaw. He then used a forklift to pick up "his" half, and drove it over to his brother's house, where he ended up staying for quite a while. But you have to wonder if he would have done the same thing if he'd actually thought things through beforehand – if he'd pictured driving down the Autobahn at 5 miles per hour with half of his house on a forklift, with drivers slowing down and pointing and major road rage going on behind him due to the huge chunks of furniture spilling out onto the road. And then he'd show up at his brother's house and get on everyone's nerves. "Honey, can you please tell your brother to get his living room out of the living room?"

In addition, experts suggest that before you start yelling, you take the time to write down what you're going to say, and rework it so that you don't say anything you're going to regret. A side benefit of this is that once you're writing it down, you can use a thesaurus to come up with much better words than the ones you were originally going to use. You'd be surprised how much better your point comes across if you use big words, and how much less the other person will argue. And then your spouse can come back a while later with what he's going to say written on a notepad, and you can read things aloud to each other, and maybe have the world's most organized argument.

My point is that anger can be very dangerous, so we should all work together to combat it. And for crying out loud, get your socks off the coffee table! And get the table out of the street!

Adventures In Columnism

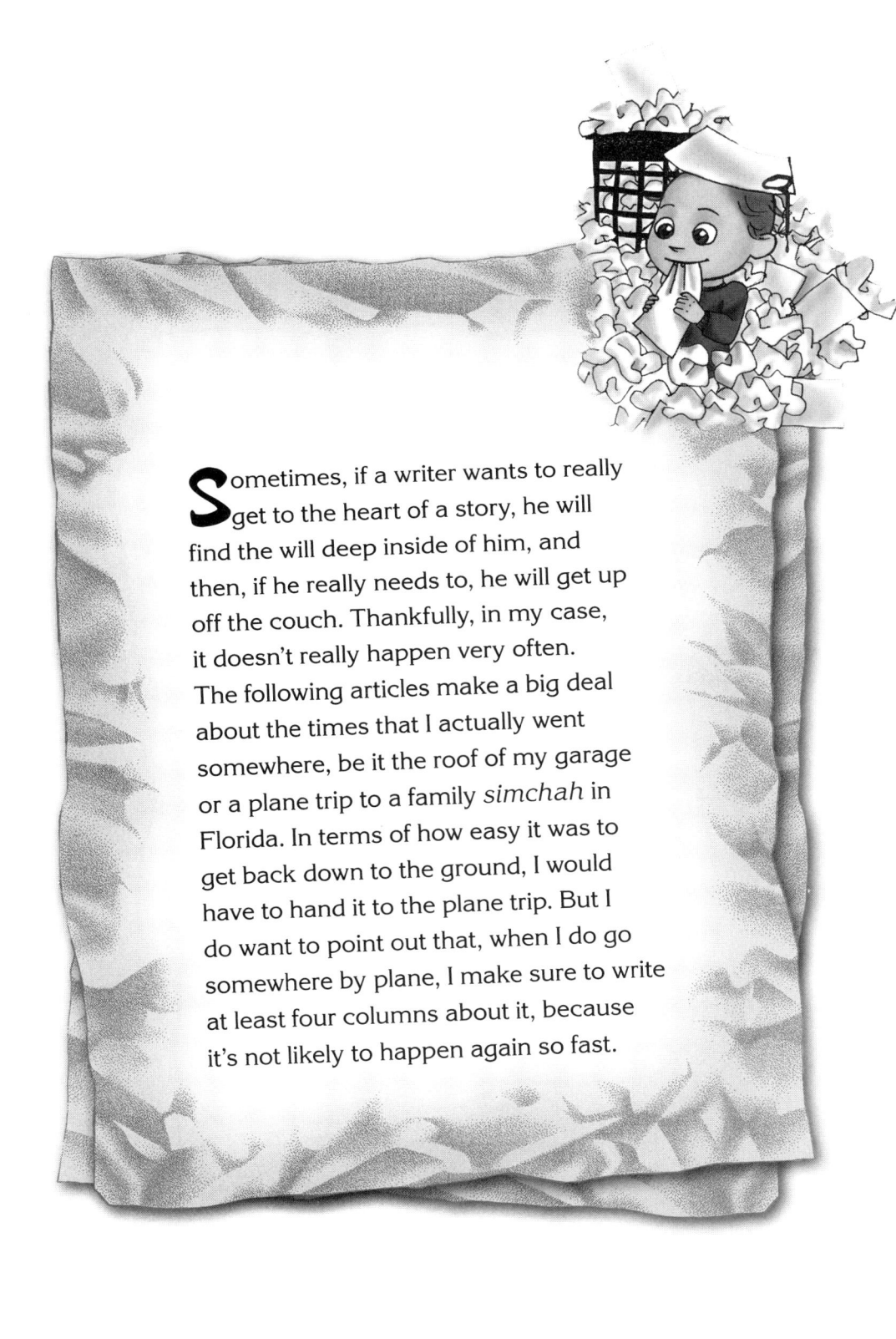

Sometimes, if a writer wants to really get to the heart of a story, he will find the will deep inside of him, and then, if he really needs to, he will get up off the couch. Thankfully, in my case, it doesn't really happen very often. The following articles make a big deal about the times that I actually went somewhere, be it the roof of my garage or a plane trip to a family *simchah* in Florida. In terms of how easy it was to get back down to the ground, I would have to hand it to the plane trip. But I do want to point out that, when I do go somewhere by plane, I make sure to write at least four columns about it, because it's not likely to happen again so fast.

If you were one of my neighbors, you'd no doubt be wondering why I spent last Thursday afternoon crouching on the roof of my garage and swatting at bees with a broomstick while a stranger in a baseball cap sprayed me in the face with insect repellent. I was doing this to protect my roofer, whose name is Jimmy. I think that if your name is Jimmy, you are legally required to work in the field of home repair. Or else you can do breaking and entering. There are very few Supreme Court Judges named Jimmy. And if you're about to undergo surgery, the last thing you want is for your doctor to say, "Hi, I'm Jimmy, and I'll be cutting you open."

My wife and I hired Jimmy because he underbid all of the other contractors by about sixty percent, and we were still trying to set aside money for the hordes of other projects that have needed to get done since we've moved into our home. Our home, like many in the Passaic area, looks like it was built by vandals as a prank in the middle of the night. It's like a bunch of teenagers were walking by, and they thought, "Hey, wouldn't it be funny if we snuck onto that empty lot and put up a house, but install everything backwards and crooked?" We think that this is why the back door of the house opens outward, so that anyone can just walk onto our porch and pop out the hinges with a screwdriver. Also, when we first moved in, our front door did not have a doorknob. Literally. There was just a gaping hole where the doorknob *should* be, and some previous owner had fixed it himself by covering the hole with duct tape.

So our first task as homeowners was to fix all of the do-it-yourself projects put in by the previous homeowners, but then at some point we ran out of money, like all of the *yeshivos*. (I think we need to set up some kind of building fund for whenever we have guests.) We have since made a list of what still needs to be fixed, and we had almost saved up enough money for the first item on the list, which was to build a floor for our front entranceway (right now our entranceway consists of a concrete-lined pit that ranges in depth from four inches to about a foot, because it's not exactly level either), when my wife noticed that all of the junk in our detached garage was getting wet when it rained, and we had to bump the entranceway down to number two. I was against this. My argument was that it didn't matter that everything was getting wet, because if we didn't have a garage we probably would have stored most of that stuff outside anyway.

Nevertheless, my wife brought in a series of contractors who talked about mold and wood rot, and basically said straight out that if we did not write them a sizeable check immediately, then it would not surprise them one bit if the entire roof would come crashing down before they'd even backed all the way out of the driveway. But then we found Jimmy. Jimmy took the job, but forgot to mention that he was deathly afraid of bees. In fact, he later told us that one time he was running away from a bee and he almost fell off the roof.

It's very inconvenient to be afraid of bees if your profession is climbing around on rooftops. Bees love building hives in moldy roofs -- it's their favorite spot, aside from under bunkhouses and behind air conditioning units. Some worm probably sells them the location, and the bees have no idea that it already belongs to someone else. So when people start climbing around on the roof, the bees get confused and angry, like they just found out that they were sold the Brooklyn Bridge. It's like in biblical times, when there were giants roaming the Earth, and a bunch of people would settle into a nice town, and then one day Og Melech HaBashan would pick it up to throw it at Moshe. "What's going on?" the people of the neighboring towns would ask each other. "What happened to Bashan?"

One of the first things Jimmy noticed, when he was about halfway finished shingling our roof, was that his original estimate was wrong, and that the problem was worse than he expected. In general, about fifty percent of the average underbid handyman's salary comes from telling people that their original estimates were wrong. They figure that at that point the homeowner will just agree to pay whatever they ask for, because otherwise these homeowners will be stuck trying to convince one of the more expensive guys to come in and finish the job, which no contractor wants to do, because for some reason they believe it is like using the previous contractor's toothbrush. But we weren't about to use up all of our entranceway money on the garage, so my wife bargained him down about a hundred dollars, and then he said that he'd knock off another seventy-five if one of us would pry the old shingles off the remaining portion of the roof.

My wife, of course, refused to go up on the roof, because going up on the roof is something that women will generally refuse to do. Nevertheless, my wife told Jimmy that *I* would be happy to do it, because what happened was, she looked over at me and IT IS NOT MY FAULT THAT WRITING IN FRONT OF A COMPUTER DOES NOT LOOK LIKE WORKING.

So I found myself up on the roof with a hammer and a broomstick. The hammer, of course, was for prying up shingles and testing portions of the roof for safety, and the broomstick, according to Jimmy, was for sweeping the dirt off the roof so that my shoes would get more traction, but I used it mainly to swat at the bees.

Jimmy and I had different approaches to walking around on the roof. My approach was the "Hug The Roof For Dear Life And Keep Saying Shema" method, while Jimmy used the "Walk Around Like You're Safely On The Ground" method. Jimmy thought I was hilarious.

"You scared of heights?" he asked.

"No," I said. "I'm just scared of falling."

"Ha ha!" he remarked.

"Very funny," I said. "There's a bee on your shoulder."

Mabul in the Garage

The key, Jimmy said while dodging insects, was to never let yourself forget that you're on a roof. This was not a problem for me. "I'm on the roof," I thought to myself. "I'm on the roof. Imontheroof, Imontheroof, *oy gevalt*, Imontheroof!"

"Why is Tatty on the roof?" my kids wanted to know.

"Get off the ladder!" I yelled. Being stuck on top of your garage really brings out your Tatty instincts.

At some point, I actually put my foot through the roof. "Is that your knee?" my wife wanted to know, from inside the garage.

"If I hit the ground," I told her, "I want 'I SAVED SEVENTY-FIVE DOLLARS' carved into my tombstone."

Eh. At least I got a column out of it.

Nearsighted

When I was a kid, someone told me that when Mashiach comes, we're all going to find everything that we ever lost. I was very excited when I heard this, because I figured I would finally find my undershirt.

I had lost my undershirt in a summer day camp in Brooklyn a couple of years earlier. The camp used to take us swimming at the Y, because, aside from the Y, there are really no other pools in Brooklyn, and one day, after coming out of the pool, I had the bright idea, seeing as it took me an exorbitant amount of time to get dressed on my own, that I would not bother putting on my undershirt, because no one can see whether you're wearing an undershirt anyway. So I put it into my bag along with my towel, or so I thought, and when I got home I realized that the undershirt was missing. So I was really excited at the prospect that, when Mashiach comes, I would finally get my undershirt back. Although at this point, I don't think it will fit anymore. But I can probably use it for polishing silver or something.

Sleep-away camp in particular is a very popular place to lose clothes – everyone loses at least one suitcase worth. Most mothers are happy if, out of the three bags they pack for their child, he comes home with at least one. And you'd think that with all these kids losing clothes, some of them would at least be coming home with *extra* clothes. But this doesn't happen. So where does it all go? The camps do have a lost and found, but there's nothing in there that has gotten lost in the last five years. Hopefully, we'll find out the answer when Mashiach comes.

Or maybe we'll find out sooner. I heard an interesting story at a *shalom zachor* I just went to for the son of a friend of mine, who also happens to be a humor writer, but I will not mention his name because the last time I asked him, he was still not sure if he wanted me to use it.

"Only if you don't write anything bad about me," he said.

Anyway, I decided that I should walk over to his house to provide some moral support in the form of eating his food and singing off key, and also to see if he still had that book that I'd lent him over two years ago. Don't you hate it when people borrow something from you, and they keep it so long that they begin to forget that they even borrowed it?

I think it's actually my cousin's book.

Once I got to the *shalom zachor*, I realized that I didn't actually know anyone there, aside from for the host, but after I'd downed about two plates of chickpeas and some leftover Pesach cake (they weren't sure exactly when the baby would be born), in walked Rabbi Jacobs (which is not his real name). Rabbi Jacobs is a big-time *mashgiach*, who flies all over the country to pop in on factories unannounced, as well as to look at cows, who don't really care what his name is. Rabbi Jacobs also runs a *shteeble* out of his basement that is so *heimish* that there is no separate entrance for the shul, so everyone has to trek snow through his kitchen and make small talk with the *rebbetzin*. ("Something smells good. Hot kiddush?")

Rabbi Jacobs told over a story about the time he was at the Y (these stories always seem to happen at the Y), and he came out of the pool to find that his glasses were missing from his locker. Also, his undershirt felt exceptionally snug. (Okay, that part isn't true.)But then a couple of weeks later, he came out of the pool to find that his wallet was stolen. At this point, I probably would have stopped going swimming. Who knew what they would have taken next? ("Hey, what happened to my up-hat?")

About three months later, Rabbi Jacobs was sent out to the middle of nowhere to check on some cows. Cows love the middle of nowhere – the grass, the wide, open spaces, the fingers pointing at them out of car windows, etc. So he did some research into rental cars in order to figure out which company had the best rates. Most people don't think about their rabbis doing regular, everyday things like shopping for cheap rental cars, or waiting in line at the DMV, or sitting on hold with customer service, or swimming at the Y, but they do.

Nearsighted

After some shopping around, Rabbi Jacobs decided to go with Budget Rent-A-Car, but when he got there, he was told that they did not have any economy cars left, and that they would bump him up to a luxury car. So he peered into the windows of all of the luxury cars to see which one had the lowest mileage, and that was the one he decided would give him the least amount of trouble driving around on a farm.

On the way out of the airport, Rabbi Jacobs came up to an intersection at which he had a green light, but as he was driving through it, a car coming from his left ran a red light and cut right in front of him. The rabbi slammed on his brakes, and just as he did so, he saw something slide out from under the driver's seat. He picked up the item, and lo and behold, it was his wallet, with his credit cards and pictures of his children and everything. (There was no cash, of course.)

So Rabbi Jacobs was trying to figure out why Hashem could possibly have wanted him to find his wallet – why he happened to be sent to this exact town in the middle of nowhere, where he picked this specific rental car company, where he was bumped up to a luxury car, in order to pick this specific car and leave the airport at that exact time in order to have someone go through a red light and have him almost crash into the guy because his glasses were missing.

Okay, so he'd replaced his glasses by that point, but it is still something he wonders about to this very day. He still has the wallet, and occasionally tries to ponder its purpose in this world.

"But what happened to the glasses?" everyone wanted to know.

(See, that's the difference between an optimist and a pessimist. An optimist says the glass is half full, and a pessimist says the glasses are still missing.)

"The glasses were not in the car," the rabbi said. Of *course* he checked. I wanted to ask him if he'd looked in that little glasses compartment they put over the driver's head, but I didn't think of it until I was walking home.

And speaking of finding things you never thought you'd see again, I finally found my book. It was right there, on the bookshelf in the dining room. My host even offered to lend me *another* book, but I said I wanted to reread the one I had.

Shoeless and Beltless

The first thing that I noticed when I flew out of town for a recent family *simchah* was that air travel certainly has changed since the last time I flew. After all, it's only been twelve years. How much can happen in twelve years?

An awful lot, as it turns out. For example, the last time I flew, I seem to remember my whole family accompanying me all the way to the gate. I think family members were even allowed onto the actual planes, so long as they promised to get off before the doors closed. Also, airline security was more lax back then. The one thing I remember about going through security was one of the guards asking me, "Did anyone else give you any packages to bring onto the plane?" Apparently, we were going on the honor system back then.

But nowadays, security is a lot tougher, and with good reason. In fact, airlines now suggest that you get to the airport at least two hours before your flight is scheduled to leave, so that you can wait on several different lines in the correct order and take off your shoes in front of total strangers and find out as soon as possible that your flight has been delayed.

The longest line, of course, is the one to go through security. Before my trip, a co-worker made sure to give me some mitzvah money (for *tzedakah*) so that I would be protected while traveling. I soon realized that the money was actually to protect me from security. Thanks to a bunch of selfish terrorists who are convinced that the best way to die is by plane, the airport security personnel are now suspicious of absolutely everything you are bringing onto the plane, including your own body. In fact, as far as the airlines are concerned, the safest way to operate would be for people to buy tickets, and then just stay home and wait for a phone call that the plane has arrived at their destination. But if they did that, there would be no point in the plane taking off at all, and it may as well just sit around at the gate. Which is pretty much what it does already.

Going through airport security involves three basic steps. Step one is to take a whole stack of those little plastic bins that they provide for you, and put in all of your carry-on luggage, as well as everything in your pockets, and your shoes, your belt, your cell phone, your pedometer, your jacket, your glasses or contacts, and your small infants. You should fill a minimum of five buckets, which you will then attempt to carry to the conveyor belt, where

Shoeless and Beltless

they will pass through an x-ray machine so that the guard on the other side of the machine, who drinks a lot of coffee and tries to figure out what things are based on their x-ray outline (and don't worry, he's seen plenty of *tefillin* before), can ascertain that you aren't bringing anything onto the plane that he cannot identify. He later makes a list and sends it to the pilot, just in case. ("Will the passenger in seat 28C come up to the cockpit, and please bring your duct tape.")

While the guard is looking at your stuff, you get to pass, shoeless and beltless, through the metal detector, which looks kind of like a doorway to which someone has forgotten to attach a house, and shoots invisible rays into your body. These rays make sure that you did not forget to put anything into the buckets, such as your *kugelach* or your fillings, and they are perfectly harmless, according to airline personnel, although you will notice that they themselves never go through the metal detector. In fact, when no one is around, they use it to cook their lunch. So experts recommend that you go through it as quickly as possible, maybe even backing up several yards first to get a running start. This is a lot of fun to do in your socks, and may help pass the time while the guard at the x-ray machine frowns at your sandwich maker. (Like you can hijack a plane with a sandwich maker. "Alright, turn this plane around, or else I'm making sandwiches!")

If there is anything in your suitcase that the guard doesn't recognize or that makes him nervous, such as a tube of toothpaste or an alarm clock, federal law requires him and a friend to root around in your belongings like starving boars in a full dumpster. They are then required to confiscate any item that they feel is dangerous or that they think is cool. They will also confiscate all liquid items that are not sealed in zip-lock bags, which, besides for being good sense, as they are known to explode all over everything at high altitudes, is also an important security measure, as studies have shown that nervous terrorists do not have the presence of mind needed to line up the little zippers on a zip-lock bag. Or else, maybe the supermarket cards you when you buy zip-lock bags, to make sure you're not a terrorist. I don't know. My wife usually buys them.

Once you and your carry-ons make it through security, it's very important to keep the line moving, so you have to quickly hobble away from the conveyor belt with your half-open suitcase and your jacket and belt and shoes and glasses in one hand, holding up your pants with the other hand, and try to find a place to sit down and get dressed before you miss your plane.

Of course, any luggage that you actually check in doesn't have to go through security with you, but that just means you have to wait on a different line beforehand so they can weigh it. Checked suitcases are required to be 50 pounds or less, or else the airline starts charging you, so we packed some empty suitcases into our luggage in case we needed them on the way back. In fact, if security had gone through our luggage, they would have thought we were smuggling suitcases.

My wife actually did not want to check any luggage at all, because she had heard too many horror stories about people who had gotten to their destinations to find that their suitcases were smashed, or broken, or in Mexico, and then they had to stand around the luggage claim office shoeless and beltless, because they'd had the bright idea that putting all that into their big suitcases would save some time at security. I assured her that this happened

Shoeless and Beltless

to a very small percentage of travelers, and she replied that what did *I* know, not having flown in almost twelve years. So I came up with the idea to put our mitzvah money in our luggage.

We ended up getting all of our luggage back in two pieces, which is just as many pieces as we checked, *baruch Hashem*, but we had to spend over an hour crowded around the luggage belt and waiting for our luggage to come spurting out of the mysterious troll-infested tunnel, which, for a while, appeared to be connected to an entirely different airport, possibly in a different country. In fact, our luggage ended up getting there after the luggage from a flight that left from the same destination an hour after us, causing us to wonder which flight it really came in on.

Anyway, that's it for now. Next time I'll write about my actual flight, if they ever let me have my pen back.

Six Pretzels

In this piece we present the second half of our article about air travel, which was supposed to run along with the first half, but it got delayed.

As you may recall, last article discussed a round-trip flight that my wife and I took to a family *simchah*, and how we had to figure out which items to bring on board with us and be subject to security officials looking through them and possibly deciding that some of them were threatening enough for them to keep, such as my suit pants, and which items would go in the big suitcase, which would hopefully get to our destination via the big network of troll-infested suitcase tunnels that connects airports around the globe. It turned

Six Pretzels

out that we carried almost everything with us, except for the bunch of suitcases that we packed into our big suitcase, in case we'd have more stuff to fly home with. Also, I had my mitzvah money in there. It was now time to get on the plane.

Despite the fact that it had been a while since I flew, I was not at all nervous about air travel. Sure, air travel seems dangerous to the ignorant layperson, inasmuch as it involves hurtling through the air miles above the ground in a big metal tube that is held aloft by principles of physics that you do not understand. If flying is so safe, they ask, how come the flight attendants sit near the emergency exits? But in fact, statistics show that you are up to three times safer in a plane than driving along the interstate, provided you are nodding off at the wheel.

Nevertheless, when I fly, I usually like to take a window seat, because I want to know if a wing falls off. Because if it did, the flight attendants wouldn't say anything. They would probably just say that we'd hit turbulence. Turbulence is generally what they say you've encountered when your plane strikes an object in midair. You'd be hurtling along through the air when WHUMP, and clearly you have hit an airborne object at least the size of a water buffalo, and the pilot will get on the P.A. system and say, "Sorry, folks, it looks like we're encountering a little turbulence." Meanwhile they're up there frantically trying to clean water buffalo organs off the windshield.

But I forgot to mention my seat preference to my wife, who actually booked the flight, and she wanted an aisle seat. So we got one seat on the aisle, and the other right next to it, leaving the window seat to be filled by someone else, who, on both flights, turned out to be a woman. So my wife ended up sitting in the middle, and I ended up on the aisle, in coach, with my huge clown feet protruding out into the aisle, as well as into my wife's foot space, because each seat in coach is about the size of a standard child's booster seat, due to the fact that the airlines want to maximize profits by trying to squish as many people as they could into each plane, never mind what the extra weight will do to the principles of physics that we do not understand.

Once we got onto the plane and found our seats, we were shown a safety video that very few people actually watched, because if they really thought that the flight was going to crash, they would not have bothered getting onto the plane in the first place. It's not like they're going to step out of the wreckage and say, "Alright, we're halfway there. Let's rent a car."

The safety video discussed where the emergency exits were, as well as how the plane was equipped with life jackets under each seat, and four inflatable rafts, and big blow-up slides under the emergency exits that also detached from the plane, and that the seats could double as flotation devices. But to me it seemed like they went to a lot of trouble to make sure people would be safe if the plane landed in the water, even though a great portion of our flight was actually going to be over land. Shouldn't there also be hang-gliders under each seat? Or was the pilot going to aim for a lake?

Thankfully, our flights were pretty uneventful, despite the fact that, on the way home, they put us on a plane that was so old that the wheels made a loud creaking noise when they were retracted, and then again when they were deployed for landing. At least I think it was the wheels. The flight attendants wouldn't say anything. They just offered us headphones. Also, the plane rocked

Six Pretzels

back and forth a lot – I don't know if this was the fault of the pilot, or the plane, or the amount of water buffalo floating around on that particular night.

But if there was one thing that I learned over the course of the trip, it's that the airline industry clearly has no idea how long anything is actually supposed to take. I had flown a similar route before, and I knew that it would take about two hours, but my wife, who booked the flight and had read the tickets, was convinced that it would take closer to four. The airline themselves also insisted that it would take four hours. But as soon as we got on the planes (both times), the pilots got on the PA system and announced that we would be landing in two hours. Maybe there's some secret shortcut that only the pilots know, and they refuse to tell the airlines. Or maybe the airlines have figured out that, flying at a certain speed, it will take four hours to get there, but the pilots have long since agreed that there is no reason to actually fly at the speed limit. Who's going to pull them over? Plus, the less time they spend in the air, the less of a chance there is that they're going to have to deploy the emergency slides, which I'm pretty sure come out of the pilot's paycheck.

So we got to our destination early, but because the pilot hadn't mentioned this to the airlines, our gate was still occupied by another plane, and we had to wait on the tarmac until those passengers finished not watching their safety video. Then, after our flight home, we had to sit around even longer, because supposedly there was a storm somewhere, and all of the pilots at every airport around the country were watching it in fear. Pilots are deathly afraid of storms, because it limits their visibility, and they have to be able to see the occasional landmark so they could have some idea if they're headed in the correct general direction. So they had us sit on the plane for over an hour, and I was *starving*, because I had already eaten my six pretzels. Finally, the pilot announced that we were going to a different gate, to which, for some reason, we would have to be towed. I could not imagine why this was. Maybe there really *was* something wrong with the wheels.

Sharing Our Time

Recently, I made the shrewd financial decision to attend a timeshare presentation. For those who aren't sure, a timeshare is a sort of hotel suite that you own for one week out of the year, and that you coordinate with 51 other families that you don't know so that you can sleep in the same room every time you vacation, assuming you always want to vacation in the same place. Also, there are amenities, such as free parking and miniature golf (which is like real golf, only smaller, and with windmills).

I was not really interested in purchasing a timeshare, but the flyer said that if we showed up for their ninety-minute sales presentation, we would get free tickets to an amusement park, whether or not we agreed to buy one. The gist of this was that the timeshare people don't really care if they sell anything; they just want to hear themselves talk.

So I called the resort, and they asked me a bunch of questions such as whether I made a certain amount of money per year, and then they insisted that I bring my wife along. This is a normal legal precaution that they take to avoid a situation wherein you purchase a timeshare, and then you come home and tell your wife, and somehow you don't explain the benefits as well as the salesperson did, and your wife force-feeds you the contract, which may render it void. Our exit strategy, of course, was to listen to whatever the salesperson had to say, and then politely explain to him that when they'd asked if we made a certain minimum income, they had forgotten to ask how much of it went toward tuition, and that we'd rather educate our children than have them play mini golf on one coordinated week every year.

We got to the resort early in the morning, and were met by a man named Jim. Jim was the kind of person who answered every question with a story. We'd ask him a question, such as what his name was again, and instead of giving us a straight answer, he would tell us that once upon a time, someone else had asked him that very same question, and do you know what he told them? That his name was Jim.

Jim also told us that he'd been selling timeshares for over thirty years, the implication being that whatever excuses we were going to come up with as to why we would not want a timeshare could not possibly have been rolling around in our heads for nearly as long as he had been coming up with reasons that people like us *would* want a timeshare. He himself owned a timeshare, he told us. And he lived just down the block. Apparently, he was the type of guy who took his vacations not only in his own city, but in his own place of work.

Jim led us into a room full of hundreds of other couples talking to salespeople and pretending to be interested in timeshares. He started by saying that, let's say, for the sake of argument, that staying in a hotel every time we went on vacation would cost us X dollars. So we took him up on the argument thing, and we said that the hotel we were staying in was actually a whole lot cheaper than X dollars, and that if we actually had X dollars to spend on a vacation, we would not be wasting part of it in a noisy room with a man named Jim so we could save a few dollars on park tickets. In fact, when all is said and done, our vacations sometimes come out less expensive than staying home and running errands. So Jim changed his numbers, which actually proved his point a little less, but he didn't let that stop him.

"Let's say," he said, "that you go on vacation every year for the next sixty years. Do you know how much that will cost you?" We didn't know the answer to that one, but we did know that we would be paying it over sixty years. So he came up with a number that seemed pretty random to us, and then he asked us what we got when we paid for a hotel room, besides for two beds and a bunch of drawers that we weren't going to use and a coffeemaker that makes two cups of hot water, depending on how you define a cup.

So we replied that yes, hotels were definitely not ideal, but sometimes you can't let yourself think about it too much, because most of what you are in town to see actually exists *outside* your hotel room, and all of the time in your hotel room is spent either unconscious, or eating Tradition soup.

At that point, Jim lowered his voice and told us that he'd decided, based on what we'd told him, that we were definitely not cut out to own a timeshare, but that he would nevertheless continue explaining the concept, in case at some point down the road we *were* cut out to own one. So we said no thanks, we'd rather just get our tickets, and he said that he was required to keep us there for ninety minutes, which did not entirely make sense. If I were him, I would have let us go, and then spent the rest of the ninety minutes playing golf and parking for free, considering he was paying for a timeshare anyway. So this was obviously part of his sales pitch. But I didn't give it much thought, because I was too busy trying to figure out where Jim was getting his numbers.

What Jim figured out, on the back of a piece of paper, was that it came out cheaper for us to pay dues on a timeshare every month for the rest of our lives than it did to stay in hotels, not counting the original purchase price of the timeshare, which he refused to reveal to us because it was more than we spent on our regular house. I have no idea what his exact numbers were, because the human attention span these days is way less than ninety minutes. But I did notice that he didn't carry a calculator, despite what he did for a living. He also said that we wouldn't have to visit the same resort every year – some years we could trade with people at another resort for only a small additional fee, depending on how you define "small".

After more than ninety minutes we were getting a little antsy, but that was when Jim remembered, all of a sudden, that he had a resort right outside that he could actually show us! On a golf cart! That would take us further and further away from our cars! Not that he was trying to sell us anything.

Sharing Our Time

So he showed us around the resort, and my wife, who is an interior designer, pointed out several design flaws, and so Jim told us that a few years earlier a woman had asked him those very same questions, and do you know what he told her?

"A story about a woman a few years before *her*?" was my guess.

"No," he said. "I told her that, because we had resorts all over the world, she never even had to stay here."

"So why *buy* here?" my wife wanted to know. Jim didn't like that question, because he was probably asking himself the same thing about his *own* timeshare. So he gave us our vouchers, and we finally got to leave our ninety-minute presentation after about three hours. I don't think Jim had a watch either.

On my recent trip to Fort Lauderdale for a family *simchah*, my friend Ari and I wanted to try our hands Jet Skiing, so we went out to the Intracoastal Waterway. The Intracoastal Waterway is a body of water that runs through Fort Lauderdale like the canals run through Venice, with lots of little inlets that are lined with the vacation homes of very rich people who don't mind pumping water our of their basements on a regular basis.

Jet Skiing is not at all like water skiing, no matter how many people have asked me that. In water skiing, you attach two big popsicle sticks to your feet and get dragged along behind a boat, and the idea is basically to try to stay on your feet, but if your regular day-to-day fitness regimen involves sitting around an office

Mainly Airborne

or yeshivah and living off the vending machine, you spend most of the time bouncing along on your stomach and saying *Tehillim*. Parasailing is similar, except that instead of popsicle sticks, you have a giant kite strapped to your back. Whereas in Jet Skiing, you sit on a small boat that looks kind of like a floating motorcycle, and your biggest real danger, so long as you keep your distance from the other boats, is that your Jet Ski may flip over.

In fact, the Jet Ski rental people were very concerned about this. We had to listen to a whole safety lecture when we first got there on what to do if your Jet Ski flips over. It turns out that what you do is basically flip it back over. I'm glad I caught the lecture. They also told us that in the small residential inlets, such as the one in which the Jet Ski launch was located, we were not allowed to actually turn on our motors. I guess this was either because of the noise, or because none of the rich people wanted inexperienced Jet Skiers crashing through their living rooms at a hundred miles an hour. So until we got to the main waterway, we were to keep our Jet Skis on "idle", which is where the Jet Ski chugs along on no power at all, and you sit there and hope that the water is at least flowing in the right direction.

They also showed us a detailed map, which they had drawn on the page of a notebook, that told us where we could and could not go, and where we could turn on our motors, but we were not allowed to take the notebook along, so we had to rely pretty much on memory. Most of our time on the Jet Ski consisted of us saying to each other, "Did we pass the Jet Ski place yet?" "I don't know; these houses all look the same to me!"

Ari and I elected to share a Jet Ski, because it cost almost a hundred dollars for a little over an hour, plus the cost of gas, which worked out to roughly a million dollars. We went out in our baseball caps, which is the standard garb for Jews who are doing something physical and don't want to lose their yarmulkes, plus it wards off anti-Semitism by concealing the fact that you're Jewish, if they're not already tipped off by the *tzitzis* protruding from under your t-shirt and the fact that you're splitting a Jet Ski. They also suggested that we take our shoes off, which we did, and I want to point out that the safety lecture did not cover what to do if you burn your feet on the dock while you're waiting for them to finish the safety lecture.

Once we got out on the water, we discovered that Jet Skis basically have two speeds:
1. Stopped, and
2. Airborne.

We spent a lot of time airborne, with whoever was sitting in the back hanging on to the other's shoulders for dear life. Jet Skis are built aerodynamically, and it turns out that putting two people on top is like tying a mattress to the top of your car, where it is basically begging to fly off and sail majestically into oncoming traffic. We also discovered that we could not hear each other when the motor was running, so we had to stop every time one of us wanted to make an observation. ("What?" "I said, 'Wow, look at that house'!") So there is no way Ari would have known if I'd pitched backward into the water.

Once we got the hang of things, our strategy for not flipping over was that, when we saw a wave coming toward us, rather than letting it hit us from the side, which is a really bad idea on a vessel that is basically one-person wide, we drove right over the wave at high speed, launching ourselves right out of the water, and then

Mainly Airborne

hitting some turbulence and SLAMMING back down on the surface of the water.

Finally, it was my turn to drive. My stint at driving went by without incident, except for three incidents. The first was when I discovered, after forty minutes of sitting on the Jet Ski, that I still had a plastic clothes hanger stuck to my life jacket. Thank goodness. I thought I was too big for the jacket. We discovered this while we were switching places, which is very hard to do without tipping over. We had to time it perfectly. I would go forward and to the left, and Ari would go backward and to the right. But in mid switch, my hanger got caught on his life jacket, and there we were, out in the middle of the waterway, struggling to detach ourselves from each other before our Jet Ski died from embarrassment and flipped over. I later wondered how many rich people saw us flying past their second story windows and wondering what was up with the guy with the hanger sticking out of his life jacket.

Our second mishap occurred when we stalled out in the middle of the water. One of the Jet Ski guys rode over and tried to help, but he didn't have any equipment, so he suggested we just idle back to the launch. But then about ten minutes later, our Jet Ski started up again. Apparently, it just needed a nap. I wish cars worked like that.

Our third mishap was when I lost my cap in midair as we flew over a wave. The Jet Ski guy, who didn't even have a chance to go back to the launch, caught it and tossed it back. But before I could catch it from him, the wind grabbed hold of it (this is *my* story, and I say the wind grabbed hold of it), and it landed in the water. So Ari and I had to scoop it up, which was very hard to do, because every time he leaned out, we almost flipped over. So we had to time it just right, with Ari leaning one way to scoop up the cap, and me leaning the other way in order to balance out the weight. We looked like two people on a tandem bicycle arguing over which way to turn.

We ended up getting back to the launch after our time was up, but the attendant vouched for us that we were a couple of bumbling tourists who had not one but *three* minor incidents happen to us, and they graciously decided not to charge us for the hanger, which needless to say, had fallen off our boat. I think they were just grateful that they didn't have to come out and help us flip our Jet Ski over. Or tow us out of someone's living room.

Who Is He?

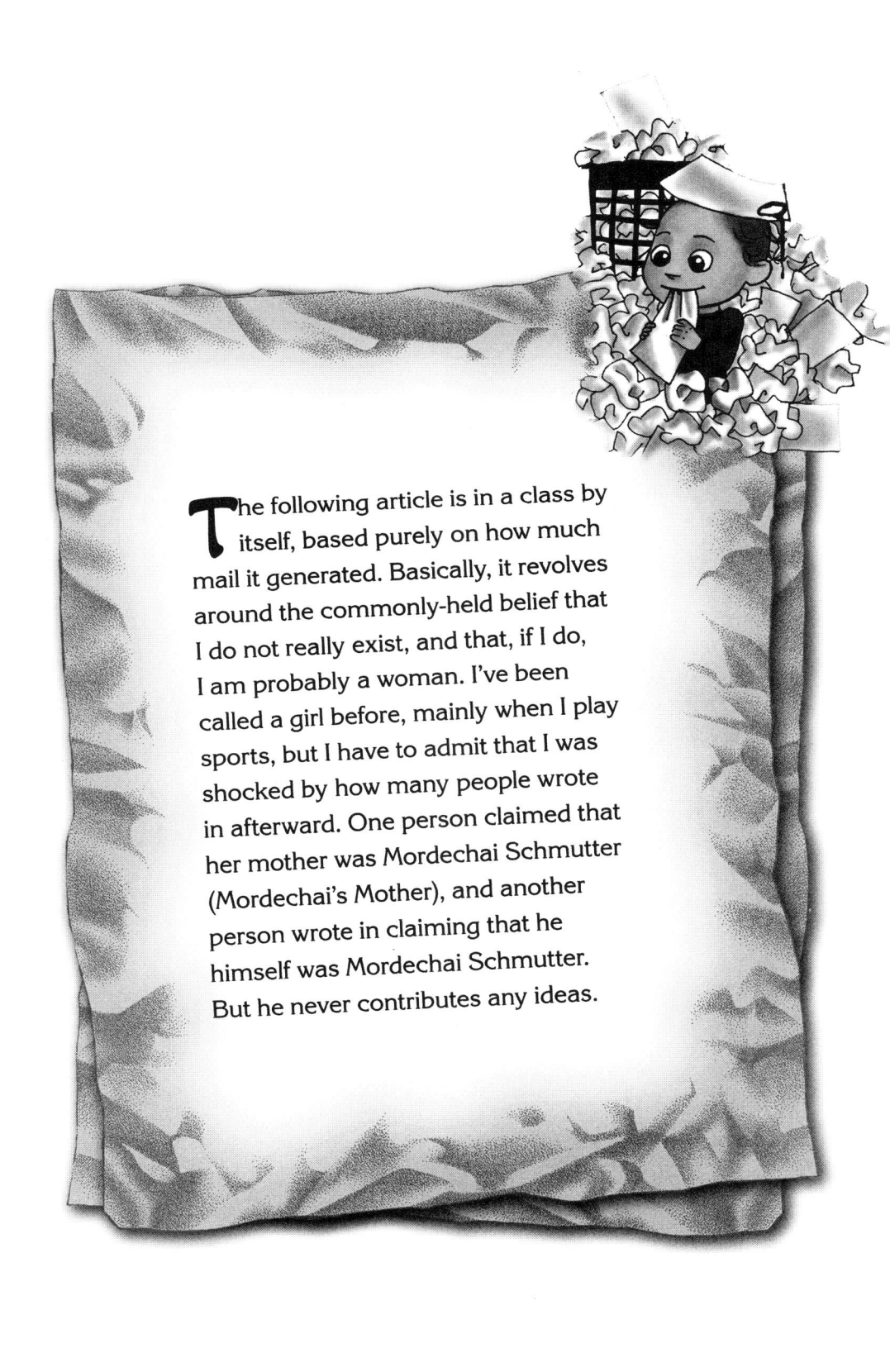

The following article is in a class by itself, based purely on how much mail it generated. Basically, it revolves around the commonly-held belief that I do not really exist, and that, if I do, I am probably a woman. I've been called a girl before, mainly when I play sports, but I have to admit that I was shocked by how many people wrote in afterward. One person claimed that her mother was Mordechai Schmutter (Mordechai's Mother), and another person wrote in claiming that he himself was Mordechai Schmutter. But he never contributes any ideas.

People very rarely believe the content of my articles. They want to know if I really put my foot through the roof of my garage, or if I forgot to bring a suit to my own Shabbos *sheva brachos*, or if I actually brought a pair of hedge clippers to my son's *upsherin*. But in all honesty, just about all of what I write is the truth. In fact, the whole point of my column is to take the whole "one day we'll look back at this and laugh" mentality, and say to my audience, "Well, why not today?"

That said, if you're ever uncertain as to whether something I've written about is authentic, ask yourself the following three questions:

1. Is it too ridiculous to be true, or is too ridiculous NOT to be true?
2. Why am I asking myself questions that the writer himself told me to ask? And:
3. What did I do with my medication?

But at least these are questions that I get all the time, unlike a letter that was recently sent to my editor. "To the Editor," it says. "I really enjoy Mordechai Schmutter's humor, but one thing is a bit confusing. I think, or rather, I *know*, that Mordechai Schmutter is not his real name; rather you should say, it's not *her* real name. I think her name is Judy Brown, as they have the same writing style. Please respond. Signed, B.K."

(At this point a lot of you are asking, "Who's Judy Brown?" But don't ask this *too* loud, because she writes for *Hamodia*, as well as for *Binah*.)

When I first read the letter, I had no idea how to respond. No one had ever come up to me and insisted that I was not who I said I was. So I checked with the *gabbai* of my shul, and it turns out that I am indeed Mordechai Schmutter. Also, I still owe some *"matanah"* for my last *aliyah*.

I will be the first to admit that almost every name I use in my articles is made up. (I have even chosen not to use B.K.'s full name, so that no one can tell whether it is a man or a woman.) And despite my being careful not to use real names, almost everyone I know has stopped sharing personal stories with me, because they're afraid that I'm going to write them down. My mother and mother-in-law in particular have become hesitant to tell stories around me, because they know that even if I don't write their actual names in my articles, I'm still going to write, "my mother," or "my mother-in-law".

But the name I use for myself is always real. Why would I use a fake name, considering that I have managed to put a free advertisement for my writing services at the bottom of every article for almost a year now?

Okay, I'll admit that "Mordechai Schmutter" sounds like it *could* be a fake name. "Mordechai" immediately conjures up images of Purim Torah, and who knows what a "Schmutter" is altogether. My mother (whose name I will not mention) used to think that it was given to our ancestor way back when they were giving out last names, and there was one lady who would not stop talking, and no one could hear their names until her son finally said, with a European accent, "Ssh, Mutter!" But my mutter could come up with theories like that, because she has consciously chosen to take on that name.

But then, a few months ago, she got a soliciting phone call from the Police Athletic League, and after she politely explained to the officer how many children she had in religious private school, the officer said, on an unrelated topic, "Schmutter... That's a German name, right?"

"Why do you ask?" my mother wanted to know. As far as we understood, my father's ancestors came from Russia.

"Oh, I'm just into all things German," the officer explained nonchalantly. "German heritage, German culture..."

My mother could not get off the phone fast enough.

But then I looked up the name, and it turns out that the Schmutter is actually a river in Germany (near Bavaria), and not a very impressive river at that. In fact, from most of the pictures I've seen, it looks like someone left a garden hose running.

But a lot of times people *will* make up names to suit their purposes. One year, when I was in Camp Gesher (this is not its real name) (it's real name is Mechaya), the counselors announced that someone named "Yoily Farloirener" had gotten lost on a trip to the bowling alley. This camp was about two blocks from the bowling alley, and it was a very hot summer, so we all pretty much *lived* there.

As I knew some Yiddish, I immediately realized that (as "farloirener" means "lost") this whole thing was an elaborate Color War breakout. But my best friend Chaim G. (that *is* his real name, but I forget his last name. Gastein? Gasman? Gasner?) was convinced, disregarding what the name actually *meant*, that Yoily was real, and that the counselors only decided to turn it into a Color War breakout after the fact. So I was wondering what the chances were that someone named "Farloirener" would get lost on the way to the bowling alley, and then I wondered about the chances of him NOT getting lost. Was getting lost in the family genes? Was there someone way back when who was always getting lost, and when they were giving out names, they decided that this was the name they would go with?

"All right, we're going to call you Farloirener. Hey, where did he go?"

"Last I saw, he was drowning in the Schmutter."

But I do have to thank B.K. for the service he (or she) has provided. You see, people are always stopping me in the street, and I never know what to say. They're like, "Are you the Mordechai

Schmutter who writes the articles?" and I say, "Yes." Then there's an awkward silence as they try to come up with something else to say, so that I wouldn't think they had nothing to say and had never really planned anything beyond, "Are you the guy who writes the articles?" Meanwhile, I'm trying frantically to think of something to say that is both spontaneous *and* funny. I should have a list of spontaneous things to say written out beforehand, so that I can just whip out the list, but I never have time to *make* a list, because I'm always behind on my articles. But it's not fair that people put humorists on the spot like that. If you're a carpenter, no one comes over to you on the street and says, "Oh, you're a carpenter? Build me a chair." Although if you're a doctor, they do ask you to look at their rash.

Now, I love an awkward conversation as much as the next guy, but I think my life would be easier if, when people were looking for Mordechai Schmutter, they were actually keeping their eyes peeled for a woman. That way, I can at least say, "You were expecting Judy Brown?"

Now, I know what B.K. is going to say. He (or she) is going to say that the fact that I just devoted an entire article to rebutting the letter just PROVES that I'm Judy. And then, on top of that, some of you readers are going to say that there is not even a B.K. to begin with – that Judy just made this all up to get a topic for her article. So there really is no way to win.

Judy Brown is a freelance writer/editor and a humor columnist for Hamodia. Feel free to write in with your comments, questions, and ideas c/o Hamodia Magazine, 207 Foster Avenue, Brooklyn, NY 11230, or email Magazine@hamodia.com.

Glossary

Afikoman – A piece of matzah that is hidden during the Pesach Seder and ransomed for presents, a tradition which is designed to keep the kids awake. Because nothing keeps you awake more than the worry of how you're going to convince your father that the larger half of his matzah is worth as much as a bike.

Aliyah (pl. aliyos) – The calling up of a person in shul to recite a blessing over the Torah. Aliyos are considered a great honor, and are often given to rabbis, guests, and people who have contributed a great deal of money to the shul, in the hopes that they will contribute more.

Aravos -- Lit., willow leaves. Aravos are used in various ways on Sukkos, including being tied into a bundle and repeatedly whacked onto the floor of the synagogue. After doing this, you will notice that some people have managed to create a pile of leaves, and their branches are stripped bare, and meanwhile your branches still have all their leaves, no matter how hard you whack them on the floor. But that doesn't mean that these people are stronger than you. It just means that they haven't been preserving their aravos properly.

Bentcher – A small booklet containing Grace After Meals that is given out as a memento at weddings, usually with a symbol stamped on the front that, if you look at it from certain angles and have had a lot to drink, kind of vaguely looks like the bride's and groom's initials. I don't know what they give out at non-Jewish weddings. Maybe *goyim* don't feel the need to carry small things out of the wedding hall in their pockets.

Chazzanus – What the chazzan chooses to do when you're starving.

A CLEVER TITLE GOES HERE

Cholent -- A hearty dish made out of beans and whatever else happens to be lying around the kitchen when you're making the cholent. It is eaten on Shabbos afternoons, and, if you are a teenaged boy, also on Thursday night, Friday night, leftover night, and scraped out of the garbage the next morning. Cholent is the teenaged boy's equivalent of a high-fiber cereal.

Dreidel – A top, which, despite the song, is almost never made out of clay.

Erev -- Lit. eve, usually referring to the day before Shabbos or a major holiday. The tradition on these days is to wait until the very last minute, and then to rush around in a panic.

Fleishig – 1. A meat dish; 2. A person who has just eaten a meat dish. (Ex., "Don't eat him; he's fleishig.")

Gabbai – The person who runs the shul. The gabbai gives out *aliyos*, arranges the seating on Yom Kippur (Where are all these people the rest of the year?), and knows, without even opening the ark, exactly which Torah scroll you should take out, and which side of the ark it's on.

Gelt – One of the most important aspects of Judaism.

Hamantaschen – Eaten on Purim, the hamantasch is a triangular cookie shaped like Haman's hat. It is unclear, though, why we eat Haman's hat. We don't eat Pharaohtaschen on Passover. Maybe it's because they're *chametz*.

Lulav – A palm branch waved in all directions on Sukkos. The tip of the lulav must not be bent or split, so the key, once you accidentally bump it into your *s'chach* a few times, is to just try not to think about it.

Makkas Bechoros – The plague that broke the Pharaoh's back.

Mashgiach – One who supervises. (Ex. "You're not gonna help? What are you, a mashgiach?")

Glossary

Matanah – a gift; usually a pledge made after an *aliyah* by a person who doesn't want the *gabbai* announcing to the rest of the shul how little he's giving.

Mechutanim – Your child's in-laws, who are not known for their generosity or their people skills.

Morah – A female teacher, usually named "Rivky".

Mashul – a parable, usually involving a king who had a son who misbehaved. You'd think that all these kings would keep their sons on a shorter leash, considering these kids may one day end up running the entire country.

Motza'ei Shabbos – Saturday night. Many have the custom to eat pizza.

Pekeleh – a bag of candy given to children at celebratory events, because if there were no bag, the kids would carry all of it home in their mouths.

Pesach – A holiday on which we celebrate our freedom from Egyptian bondage by cleaning our houses and eating matzah. But the most important thing to remember about Pesach is: *Don't Yell "Challah" in a Crowded Matzah Bakery. By M. Schmutter.*

Purim – a holiday on which we get drunk and give each other food baskets, but not in that order.

Rebbetzin – The rabbi's boss. Must know how to make an awesome cholent.

Sar Ha'ofim – The chief baker. In Genesis, Pharaoh finds a rock in his bread and sentences the Sar Ha'ofim to spend time in prison, where you find things in your bread that you *hope* are only rocks.

Shabbos – The Day of Rest, which falls out once every seven days, usually on a Saturday. We eat festive meals, go to shul, and take a long nap (at home, not in shul).

Shalom Zachor – A party, usually in the home of someone whose wife is in the hospital with a newborn, where men show up and celebrate the fact that they were able to get out of the house on a Friday night.

Shavuos – A holiday commemorating the giving of the Torah. We eat cheesecake, and then we stay up all night. But not because of the cheesecake.

Sheva Brachos – A series of parties that take place for the entire week after a wedding, during which the bride and groom have to eat pareve ice cream and pretend that they're still as excited about the parties as the people who are sick of coming to them hope that they are.

Shteeble – like a shul, but smaller, and in someone's basement.

Shul – like a *shteeble*, but bigger, and with membership fees.

Simchas Torah – A holiday on which we celebrate the reading of the entire Torah by dancing and then eating stuffed cabbage and then coming back and dancing, but a little slower this time.

Sukkah – a temporary booth put together by Jewish men, who are not known for their building skills, and held up by prayer.

Sukkos – A holiday devoted to commemorating the period, thousands of years ago, when our forefathers traveled through the desert on the way to the promised land, and, every time they stopped to rest, they put up temporary huts and ate chicken soup with their coats on.

Yom Tov – (Pronounced "*Yuntiff*".) A holiday. A time for growing spiritually, until your pants don't fit.

Zeeskeit – a term of endearment for your kids. (Ex., "Zeeskeit, what is my toothbrush doing in the bathtub?")

Mordechai Schmutter writes a weekly humor column for *Hamodia*, which is syndicated in one other magazine around the country. He also attempts to teach Language Arts to a bunch of high school guys, most of whom are usually too upset that he showed up on any given day to even pay attention to his lessons. He is also the author of the book, *Don't Yell "Challah" in a Crowded Matzah Bakery*. He lives in New Jersey with his wife, his kids, and some furniture.